PETER J. MORRIS

7,240 Miles to Feed His Sheep

An Ordinary Boy Sent to Do Extraordinary Things

Peter J. Morris is the Executive Director of International Programs and Associate Professor of Japanese History at the University of Shiga Prefecture. Peter served a mission for the Church of Jesus Christ of Latter-day Saints (the Mormons) in the Japan Fukuoka Mission. The experience of serving a mission has helped him to have a desire to readily share his testimony, as well as serve in various capacities in the Church both at home in the States, and back in Japan.

This book is dedicated to
my wife, my parents,
and of course, my greatest joy:
Erika, Eddy, Elina, Ernie, and Emmie

Preface

"Simon, son of Jonas…", Jesus inquired, "… lovest thou me?" When I read of this passage in Matthew, I can imagine that vivid scene on the shores of the Sea of Galilee where Jesus challenges Peter, his most dedicated and loyal disciple. This is Peter, who if only for a moment, walked on water with the Savior; the same Peter who turned his back on what many might have considered a lucrative business to devote his entire life to following Him. As they traveled about, Peter witnessed the countless miracles that were performed by Jesus. Through his Priesthood power, Peter too would perform miracles.

In protection of the Master, Peter smote off the ear of the high priest's servant as Jesus was put under arrest at Gethsemane. Peter suffered alongside the others as they watched their Lord being not only scourged, but brutally nailed to the cross. In order to avoid a similar punishment, Peter suffered the betrayer's shame by denying his association with the Son of God; the depth of his disgrace was soon manifested as he "wept bitterly"[1]. At last, Peter experienced the wonder of the arrival of the resurrected Christ, receiving the charge, "Go ye therefore and teach all nations, baptizing them in the name of the Father, and of the Son, and of the Holy Ghost".

---

[1] Matt. 26:75 and Luke 22:62

In spite of his calling, time passes and Peter returns to his fishing business. A man appeared on the shore where Peter and others were out on their boat. Peter soon realized that the man was the resurrected Jesus. Without a thought, the elated Peter threw himself into the water and swam to the shore to greet Him. In the evening, as Jesus broke bread and fish for his disciples, He inquired of Peter not once, but three times, whether or not he truly loved Him. By the third time the perplexed Peter emphatically answers, "Lord, thou knowest all things; thou knowest that I love thee."[2] As he had done the previous two times, Jesus replied to Peter with, "Feed my sheep". With this re-clarification of his duty, Peter begins a life-long mission, to continue spreading the word of Jesus Christ and to nurture the Master's flock here on Earth.

Holding the proper Priesthood keys, Peter led the Church of Jesus Christ, which flourished among the Gentiles over the following sixty years or so. Nevertheless, those keys would be lost from the earth.

With James and John, Peter restored the Priesthood keys which were necessary to restore the Gospel in these the latter days. I am honored to share my name with the senior apostle Peter. I know I still have a very long journey ahead of me if I ever want to possess the kind of understanding that Peter had regarding the divine nature and mission of our

[2] John 21: 17

Savior. However, the journey thus far has continually defined and redefined my testimony of Him.

In the waning years of my high school career, my dad somehow put in his mind that our family needed to raise sheep of all things. Throughout my growing up years, we maintained what most people might consider a "hobby farm". We started with a few beef cows and chickens; later on, we bought a couple of pigs, some geese, a milk cow, and even a turkey or two. We never really became attached to any of the livestock; although we did name our two pigs "Percy" and "Petunia". Yet however endearing their names may sound, this never took away from the enjoyment that came from eating the delicious ham, bacon, and pork chops that they provided us.

I don't think that any of us considered ourselves farmers. Our chores in the barn went right alongside cleaning our rooms and making our beds. The animals were as much a food source as the groceries we bought at the store. Several months after Dad bought the sheep, I found myself in a situation that would narrow whatever distance I had been able to put between myself and those farm animals. It all happened one Saturday morning.

We were all roused out of our beds by unfamiliar noises outside, accompanied by Dad's shuffling footsteps across the floor upstairs. I rushed up the stairs in time to see Dad slip out the back porch door with a rifle in his hand. As I scrambled to get my shoes on, I heard him discharge a couple of rounds. By the time I made my way outside, Dad was already coming towards the house with something in his arms. It was one of the new lambs. He told me to run and get an old towel.

It turned out that a couple of coyotes had gotten into our pasture. One of them managed to secure a good grip on the back of the poor little thing, but was then forced to release her in order to escape Dad's twenty-two caliber wrath. The damage to the lamb was pretty severe. As the two of us inspected the deep slashes in her flesh, Dad made the decision that she should be put down. I began to protest, begging for him to take her to the veterinarian, who was nearly thirty minutes away. Although she was losing a lot of blood, the little lamb seemed quite alert. Reluctantly, Dad gave in to my pleas and we loaded up into the truck and headed for town.

After about sixty stitches and a dose of antibiotics, we brought our little wooly patient home. There were no promises that she would survive, but we were given a vial of antibiotics and a supply of bandages. It turned out that it would now be my responsibility to try and nurse the little lamb back to health. Each day, before and after school I had the task of administering the shots and re-wrapping her bandages. I brought her mother in for a little while each time so she could nurse. She even began to eat grain out of my hand. After a week or so, when we were confident that she would actually survive the trauma; Dad and I went ahead and named her Martha. It may have been because she was born on George Washington's birthday, or we named her after Dad's mother.

We kept little Martha in the back room of our upper shed, approximately 200 yards from the house. The entire trip could be calculated to nearly a quarter mile (rounded up). I continued to make this little journey twice a day for the following month. While her condition improved considerably, it soon became evident that there was some nerve damage. It seemed that she had lost some of the use of her hind legs. Yet in spite of that, I watched her grow stronger and stronger.

I calculate that I must have walked roughly 15 miles to take care of Martha over the course of a little more than a month. I probably devoted 60 hours of my time, feeding her and tending to her wounds. Notwithstanding her disabilities, she was eventually able to join the rest of Dad's little flock. With a little extra effort, she actually managed to keep up with the others quite well. Soon after I had left home, I learned that little Martha even went on to become a mother.

Soon after that experience I began making preparations to finish up high school and of course, go on my mission. Some of my best stories still come from that relatively short time as a missionary. I often get a chuckle when I ponder on the crazy things that we did as missionaries. On certain occasions, a tear or two can still find its way out of the corner of my eye.

Over the years, I've been able to see many other boys receive that call to serve, including my own brothers and sons. Some wholeheartedly answered it, coming back as men and ready to move upward and onward. Still others either changed their minds or came home early. It makes me sad to think of all the memories that they will never have; memories that have blessed my life and even the lives of those around me.

From about the age of ten, I had come to understand that serving a mission was not only a privilege, but actually a commandment to all the young men. President Spencer W. Kimball was the prophet at the time and his very words confirmed that understanding. In May of 1974 he said the following:

> The question is asked: Should every young man fill a mission? And the answer of the Church is yes, and the answer of the Lord is yes. Enlarging this answer we say: Certainly every male member of the Church should fill a mission, like he should pay his tithing, like he should attend his meetings, like he should keep his life clean and free from the ugliness of the world and plan a

celestial marriage in the temple of the Lord.[3]

President Kimball made it clear at least in *my* mind, that unless there was an overwhelming barrier in the form of a disability or a worthiness problem, all LDS young men were simply expected to become worthy and then serve an honorable mission.

Throughout my years growing up, I was often inspired by Brother Dickson, a man in our small stake. At the young age of 35, he was called to be the President of the Mexico North Mission. We all thought how amazing his calling was; because we knew that he had also served his mission in Mexico. Brother Dickson shared some of the most inspiring stories in regards to that first mission call, his strong desire to serve a mission, and the incredible challenges that he was faced with.

Brother Dickson, like many LDS boys, grew up in preparation for his mission. He submitted his paperwork on time, and then awaited his call. I imagine that he was surprised and excited to learn that he would be going to Mexico. But as it turned out, his excitement was somewhat short lived, when he learned from his doctor that he had bone cancer in his right arm; it would have to be amputated. The doctor further warned that even after removing the arm, the cancer could still

[3] The Ensign: May 1974, pg. 86

prove to be fatal; so serving the mission was not advisable.

I have often wondered how I would have coped with such a dilemma. Yet the most inspiring part of his story to me as a boy was that Brother Dickson was still determined to answer the call and serve his mission in Mexico. He told us how, as a former right-hander, getting ready for his mission became an entirely new kind of test. In his own words, "Everything was a challenge: tying shoes, buttoning shirts, carrying large objects, driving, shaving, drawing, eating, being stared at, enduring phantom pain, and so on."[4]

I feel very privileged to have heard this story in my youth, years before Brother Dickson related it in the New Era in 2002. His testimony no doubt inspired me in my own preparations. Prior to leaving on my mission, I had already learned to tie my own necktie, just as Brother Dickson did; but I can't imagine having to do it with one hand.

Even these many years later, Brother Dickson's stories have remained with me. Today Elder Dickson[5] continues to be an example of determination and drive. He refused to let his own challenges detour him from doing his priesthood duty and serving the Lord. While Brother Dickson's situation may seem somewhat rare, there are so many boys who have allowed

---

[4] The New Era: February 2002
[5] Elder John B. Dickson currently serves in the First Quorum of the Seventy

even the most trivial of distractions or doubts get in the way of what they should do.

Among the numerous callings in all the wards and branches I have lived in over the years, I have had the opportunity to spend much of my time working with the youth and more particularly, the young men. On more than one occasion, some of these boys have voiced their opinion that serving a mission is an inconsequential choice, which was theirs alone to make. I of course acknowledged that yes; we are all blessed with the sacred gift of agency. But then I would follow that comment with President Kimball's aforementioned remarks. Sometimes I would go even further to add the fact that those words didn't go away with President Kimball.

Nearly ten years after President Kimball's statement, President Benson reiterated those very words and then added:

> As a young man, are you earnestly preparing to serve a full time mission? The Lord needs every young man between the ages of nineteen (now 18) and twenty-six worthy, prepared, and excited about serving in the mission field"[6]

Succeeding President Benson as the Prophet, Howard W. Hunter further added, "Earlier prophets have taught that every able,

[6] The Ensign: May 1988, pg. 84

worthy young man should serve a full-time mission. I emphasize this need today."[7]

Our most recent past prophet, even Gordon B. Hinckley lovingly clarified that there is a sense of duty that should be fostered in the hearts of every worthy young man in the church. In 2002 President Hinckley said:

> I am not suggesting that He will withdraw His blessings and leave you bereft if you do not go on a mission. But I am saying that out of a spirit of appreciation and gratitude, and a sense of duty, you ought to make whatever adjustment is necessary to give a little of your time consecrating your strength, your means, your talents to the work of sharing with others the gospel, which is the source of so much of the good that you have.[8]

Elder Jeffery R. Holland culminated the words of the prophets when, after describing the plan and intentions of Satan to stop the work, he unequivocally expressed the need for every young man to step up and serve:

> But apparently his effort to stop the work will be reasonably well served

[7] The Ensign: November 1984, pg. 87
[8] The New Era: October 2002, pg. 5

> if he can just bind the tongue of the faithful. Brethren, if that is the case, I am looking tonight for men young and old who care enough about this battle between good and evil to sign on and speak up. We are at war…[9]

So you see, it is as clear to me now as it ever was before that, while preparing for and serving a mission is the personal choice of every young man or woman, it is what our Father in Heaven wants and even expects us to do. Perhaps it wouldn't even seem a choice to the young men, if they understood that much of the responsibility to bring others unto Christ rests largely upon their shoulders. We are the very Gentiles that Nephi saw in a vision; those who are to gather Israel bearing those "plain and precious things" (the restored gospel) which had been taken away from the earth for generations.[10]

I owe so much to the wonderful experience of having served a mission. It was certainly a pivotal point in the building of my own testimony of the Gospel. Nevertheless, even upon my return from serving in Japan, I would sometimes wonder, "Did I really make a difference?" or "Was I a good enough missionary?"

---

[9] October General Conference Talk, 2011

[10] 1 Nephi 13

Some years back, when our family was comprised of just four members (now seven) and living in Japan. We had briefly returned home to the States in order to give a baby blessing to our new son Eddy, in addition to spending Christmas with my family. Upon arrival, my mom handed me a stack of mail which had been accumulating over the course of several months. Most of it was junk mail, but there were also a few letters included.

Among these letters was a very "triffy" envelope. Now the word Triff was a term that we used on my mission all the time. It meant a girl who, let's just say, "liked" the missionaries. Quite often we would get letters or notes on this type of "cutesy" stationery. I later learned that the term "Triff" was derived from the John Wyndham novel, *The Day of the Triffids.*

In the story, Triffids were carnivorous plant-like creatures that were capable of blinding and killing people. Ironically, that was often an appropriate description of some of those cute young women, whose flirtations could potentially be a distraction to some of us missionaries; although I am pretty certain that the majority of those girls didn't even realize their effect. This type of envelope was very typical of what any missionary in Japan might find in the mailbox once in a while. Yet in this case, the sender's name on the envelope didn't ring a bell with me.

I opened the envelope and pulled out the matching stationery. Of course the letter was written in Japanese. Although I had been living in Japan, and was considered by some to be quite proficient in both the written and spoken Japanese word (for an American); this particular "female" style of handwriting was difficult for me to decipher. Fortunately, my curious wife Takeko was looking on and began reading it aloud to me. The message, loosely translated read something like this:

> Dear Elder Morris,
> I hope this letter gets to you alright, as I know it has been a while. So many things have changed since I last saw you. I graduated from high school and have since moved out and am now at a nursing school in Nagoya. I have never forgotten all that you and Elder Nakamura taught me. And I never stopped reading the *Book of Mormon* that you gave me. I'm writing you to tell you about something that happened to me some time ago. I was walking along on the street and saw the Mormon missionaries. I immediately thought about you and went over to greet them… To make a long story short, I was recently baptized a member of the Church. Now I am on my own and finally getting to do what I know is right for me. Thank you for all that you and Elder Nakamura did for me. I will never forget you.

A rush of emotion poured over me as I realized who this person was. Her name was Yuka. My companion and I had taught her in the area of Omuta, Japan. At that time, I was one of two Americans in a four-man apartment that covered an entire area of approximately a hundred square miles. That area was and is, without a doubt my favorite place. I was there for a little over five months.

Yuka was a shy girl that we knew from one of the English classes that I was teaching. She had a real interest in learning English and attended the class that we offered at her high school. In time, she began attending our adult class on Thursdays and even our children's class on Saturday. After class on one particular Thursday night, my companion and I happened to have an appointment in the same area where Yuka lived.

We offered to ride our bikes with her down the dark streets for a while. As we pedaled along, she asked the sort of question that missionaries are always hoping to hear, "So, what is it that you guys really do all day, besides teaching English?" We only had a short distance before we were to go in a different direction, so I reached into my bag and pulled out the "Plan of Salvation" pamphlet. I handed it over to her like the baton in a relay race and then offered to talk about it after the class at her school the following week. She happily agreed.

At the school, Yuka came to my companion

and me with the pamphlet in her hand. "This is exactly what I've been looking for", she whispered, a little embarrassed that others might hear. I know, I know, this sounds so very cliché, like the story in a seminary video or something. But that's really what she said! So, over the next week or two, with her mother's permission, my companion and I began teaching her the lessons. She seemed to absorb everything we taught her. She even prayed for the first time during our first lesson. I can't begin to describe the feeling that the spirit brought to us that day. We ended that first meeting with my giving to her a copy of the *Book of Mormon*.

The following Saturday at our children's class, Yuka handed the *Book of Mormon* back to me with a serious look on her face. I asked her if there was a problem; her reply was that she had a strong feeling that she should return the book. I was a little confused and concerned. She continued, "This is a very wonderful book. I couldn't put it down, because it is so special. I knew you would need it back right away; I haven't slept or studied since I started reading, and I wanted to finish it before giving it back to you today."

Hold on! This young woman had read the entire *Book of Mormon* in only three days?! Even after an entire year of Seminary, I wonder if *I* was even able to complete it. I couldn't believe my ears. I recall the story from my seminary class when Parley P. Pratt had discovered the *Book of Mormon*. "I read all day; eating was a burden, I had no desire for food; sleep was a burden when the night came, for I preferred reading to sleep."[11] This girl had made that same wonderful discovery. To be honest, I was a little jealous. I had truly been taking for granted one of the most magnificent possessions that had always been available to me.

I then made it clear to Yuka that this copy of the *Book of Mormon* was hers to keep. I even opened my bag to show her a number of additional copies. From that point, we continued to teach her the entire lesson plan, twice. I believe that she read the *Book of Mormon* a couple more times before I was transferred. She soon developed a strong desire to be baptized. But after several discussions, even with the help of our branch president, her mother would not let her join the Church. While she would still be allowed to attend meetings and continue learning, her baptism would have to wait until she graduated from high school and out on her own.

I was truly sad. Yuka had an entire year before graduating from high school and I thought for sure she would "grow cold" and lose interest. Five or so years later, after reading her letter, I could hardly express the joy that I felt when I discovered that she had made it after all. Perhaps it was the same joy described in the verse: "And if it so be that

[11] Pratt, *Autobiography of Parley P. Pratt*, p. 44

you should labor all your days in crying repentance unto this people, and bring, save it be one soul unto me, how great shall be your joy with him in the kingdom of my Father!" [12] With that experience, I began to reflect a little more intently on the things I had done on my mission. I couldn't help but wonder if there wasn't more to my mission than I had thought. Were there others like Yuka?

I have since begun reviewing and reevaluating my mission and the events that led up to it. For some reason or another, I still keep even the tiniest scraps of paper from my mission, boxed up and stowed away. Once in a while, I'll open them up and ponder on those days, and what my mission has done for me so many years later. Nearly every day of my mission is somewhat legibly recorded in the journals that I kept. As I go through them, it is as if I am taken back in time and space.

I'd like to think that mine was just an ordinary mission, if there *is* such a thing. I didn't have the privilege of baptizing droves of people as Alma did. [13] As far as I am aware, no major miracles were performed. While I am confident that I served an honorable mission, there were certainly times when I wasn't the best of missionaries. What I do know is that the time and place of my mission was clearly determined by our Heavenly Father. For those of you who have already had the opportunity to

[12] D&C 18:15
[13] Mosiah 18

serve, you probably understand what I'm talking about. I hope you enjoy this story. I hope it spurs some of your own wonderful memories. This story is not necessarily intended to inspire anyone; but if that's what happens, so be it. Rather, this is simply an opportunity to share with you what I feel that I have gained from serving a mission.

For those yet to serve a mission, perhaps this can be somewhat educational. Mind you, this is not like a John Bytheway or Randy Bott book on how to prepare for your mission; or even how to be a great missionary. Those types of books are great books to be sure; they do a wonderful job of helping future missionaries to prepare to go. But what I can tell you is that if you only have a willing heart and the courage to let the Lord guide you, you *will* be great; of that, I have no doubt. If you are actively engaged in your scripture study, prayers, and are utilizing the tools such as "For the Strength of Youth" and "Preach My Gospel" you will already be prepared.

What I offer through this story, is a chance to come along with me to see just what kind of extraordinary things can happen to an ordinary young man or woman. I hope to share with you some of my feelings of joy, pain, disappointment, and achievement which have actually helped to create who I am.

I have come to believe that in the relatively short time that we have on this earth, any undertaking we perform in the spreading of the gospel is like tossing a stone into a still pond. One person can make a difference. One act of kindness can change a person's heart. To those of you who look back, thinking that your mission wasn't all that special; and to those who may be thinking that going on a mission won't make much of a difference. I can say, in either case, "You are mistaken".

No matter how small we think the impact of the stones are that we have either thrown, or will throw into the proverbial pond of life; I'm quite certain that, in time, we can all come to know just how far the ripples of that impact have gone. It may not even be until the life hereafter, but the outcome of our efforts will eventually become known to us. Over the course of many years following my mission, I am still learning that the work I had done there continues, even to this day.

I'm writing this little narrative, not to persuade anyone to go out and do anything per se. Although I continue to age, I'm not yet that wise old man, passing along his many years of wisdom and experience. So you may ask, what exactly *is* my motivation for writing this? Perhaps I am afraid I will somehow forget everything if I don't write it down. Nevertheless, I can't help but think that even if there is but one young man or woman who is thinking, "How will my going on a mission make a difference to anything or anyone?" The short answer might be, "perhaps it won't; that would depend on you". You can go ahead and stay home never, ever knowing the actual answer.

But let's just say that you do decide to go. And even after going, perhaps you feel that your contribution was somewhat minimal. Try to imagine, at some point later in life; if only one person should come to you and say, "Thank you for being there for me in my search for the truth." Words could not describe the joy you could share as you embrace each other as brothers or sisters in the gospel; both knowing that you did in fact make the right choice by serving the Lord on a mission.

When the little lamb Martha needed me so badly, I suppose that I thought myself a compassionate, self-sacrificing individual. After all… my father and I did rescue her form the very jaws of those wolves (well coyotes anyway).[14] I had mentioned that, under my dad's direction, I walked some 15 miles over several weeks with the charge of taking care of that one little sheep.

I suppose that I considered it a big deal… all the time that I devoted to her. I was so happy and proud to know that little Martha would eventually be alright, especially after all that I had supposedly "sacrificed" for her. It would only be a short while till I would travel some 7,240 miles to attend to the sheep of another fold, the sheep of the Good Shepherd. I only wish that I knew then, as I know now, how important that task was to be. If I *had* known, I might have worked a little

---

[14] Alma 5:59

harder and prepared a little more. Nevertheless, I am thankful to the Lord for issuing that call to me; and that I was further blessed with whatever it took inside of me to answer it.

Chapter 1: Growing Up

I grew up on a small island in the Puget Sound in Northwest Washington State. We moved there from California when I was eight. I was the only one of 5 boys not born in California; because for a short while, the family moved to Virginia for Dad's work just in time for me to be born. But it wasn't long until the family was back to California… Lakewood California.

I recall many things about Lakewood. I remember some of the good friends in our neighborhood. One of my best friends, since before we even started school, was a boy named Bobby. I seem to remember when we were about four or five; Bobby ate a whole spoonful of dirt, claiming that it had important minerals in it. Until the first grade, we were always together either at his house or ours. Bobby's family happened to be Catholic. I could see that they were very close and loved each other. But somehow I felt that some things at his house were a little different than at ours. Nevertheless, that never seemed much of an issue, because we were really good friends.

We spent a lot of time with the kids in the neighborhood. For some reason they all liked to hang out at our house; my parents were always fine with that. Across the way was another family with two girls that were close in age to us. Soon after we moved away, that family ended up joining the Church. I would hope that over the seven or eight years we were there, our family helped to contribute to that somehow. In the warm California weather, the neighbor kids would often come to our house to swim in our pool. We swam from about the beginning of March to the end of October, non-stop. Of course Mom was always around to supervise. She taught all of us how to swim.

That pool in our back yard is likely the reason we ended up leaving Lakewood. It's the scene where my parents' world appeared to crash down around them. This is one memory of that house that I still dream about from time to time. I was the youngest in our family, until about the age of five; until my mom became pregnant and had yet another baby boy, Preston. His birth came shortly after I started Kindergarten, and he left us just about a month before his second birthday.

It was morning; Mom was busy in another room, while we entertained ourselves in front of the TV. The details of that morning are a little fuzzy now; but what is clear, is how my brother and I found our little brother, lifeless at the bottom of the pool. As a dad, I find it difficult to imagine how any other six or seven-year-old might have reacted to such a scene. In my mind, I can still hear our frightened screams. In a matter of seconds, we watched our mom fearlessly dive to the bottom of that 10-foot deep pool, pull Preston's precious little body out, and try desperately to revive him. I can still hear the blaring sirens as they neared our house. In my mind's eye, I can see Mom and the baby riding off in the ambulance.

It's only now, after having children of my own, that I think I can somewhat understand the loss that my Mother and Father must have felt. I would gladly sacrifice myself than have to watch one of my own children leave this world in such a way. I recall the months of agony that my family endured after that day. At the funeral, my brothers and I carried little Preston's casket. There was a lot of crying in our house.

Some years later, I was told that Bobby's mother had come to my mom to express her sympathies. In spite of her own church's beliefs regarding un-baptized babies, she let my mom know that she sincerely believed that our family would be united with Preston again.

It wasn't long until my parents decided that our house carried too many sad and scary memories; we eventually packed up and moved to Washington State. Up in Washington, life would be very different from anything we had ever known. As far as the Church in the area was concerned, the members there had only recently become a dependent branch. It was strange to us, being amongst so few members. The meetings were first held at an old brick building formerly used as a bank. Until my mission, I couldn't imagine another place in the world with so few people holding so many Church callings.

As my brothers and I grew, so did our little branch. We moved from that bank to the larger, local Masonic Hall on Sundays, and other days when they weren't using it. But eventually we outgrew that location and moved to the old, uninhabited high school on the hill, just above the new one. My closest friend, Jeff and his family moved in when I was in 5th grade.

The two of us held the brunt of the Aaronic priesthood duties much of the time. There was a significant gap in ages between us and the older boys. As deacons, we passed the sacrament each week. With the addition of another close friend named Glenn, as teachers we prepared and cleaned up the sacrament trays, in addition to passing the sacrament of course.

Over the next few years, as more families moved to the area, our branch continued to grow. By my second year in high school, with a lot of hard work and sacrifice, our branch would finally become a ward; we were ready for our own meetinghouse.

Those were the days when the members were required to come up with a significant amount of the cost before the Church would allow them build a chapel. I can remember the announcements at the pulpit each week, "please remember the building fund." During this time, the community around us had been growing as well. As a result, the demand for new housing also increased. This attracted many new builders and skilled carpenters. Many of these emigrants also happened to be members of the Church. That was among the reasons why my dad chose to move there. Mom's brother Don, also a builder, brought his family there as well.

It was proposed that the branch find a way to utilize all this new talent and expertise. So, on one particular Saturday, all of the men and the young men came together to build two spec houses from which the proceeds of the sale would go towards the building fund.

On previously finished foundations, we nearly completed both houses in a single day. My brother Pat and I were sent back after school once or twice to finish the roof on one of them. To everyone's amazement, that project seemed to tip the scales, and the ward building construction was approved; what a sight to behold when it was completed. Sitting alongside the only road going on or off our island, everyone in the community finally had a clear view of the Church's presence.

During my first year in high school, our Seminary class was comprised of six seniors, a junior, a sophomore, and two freshmen. We also made up the only Church membership at our high school. The following year, there were only four boys left in our Seminary class.

Everyone who knew us at school knew that we were Mormon. On the one hand, this made it easier to back out when friends from school invited us to go out drinking, etc. Yet if you wanted to make the effort to go along, they would be all too happy to welcome you with open arms, and bottles. The only consequence to that was losing your credibility as a Mormon.

It so happened that my patriarchal blessing states that I would never be tempted to break the Word of Wisdom; and I never was. Nevertheless, my non-member friends never gave up trying to get me to come with them. Before long, they did give up on getting me drunk. They made sure I that knew that soft drinks would also be available, just for me. But for some reason or another, I would have some sort of Church activity to go to that same night; it's funny how it always seemed to work out.

Because our ward was so small, we had to get together with the other kids in the stake, if we wanted to have any fun at all. As a result, the youth in our stake became very close during those years. This was in spite of the fact that the kids in other the wards went to different high schools, sometimes even rival high schools. Ninety-five percent of the girls I managed to get a date with were from the other wards in the stake. My friends at school couldn't understand how we "un-sociable" Mormons knew so many kids from the opposing teams at football and basketball games. I was even called a traitor, because I asked a cheerleader from the other team to go out after one of our games.

Those were most definitely some of the best times of my life. We eventually developed a reputation for being a very outgoing and crazy bunch of Mormon boys. During my last two years of high school, a few more additions had moved into our ward and joined our little group of radicals. Our reputation preceded us even beyond our stake boundaries.

Our little LDS gang discovered that we

had very much in common. We all enjoyed music and singing. We favored the older bands that sang in tight harmony like The Beach Boys, The Beatles, and so on. We sang in a number of stake pageants, stake and regional choirs, and anything else we could nose our way into. We never did join any official singing groups at school, but everyone knew what we could to do. We could often be found jamming in the halls or in the cafeteria, we didn't care. In my senior year, the choir teacher even asked me if I could form a quartet to sing at the baccalaureate service before commencement.

I made many wonderful and long-lasting friendships with members and non-members through our mutual love for music and drama. Throughout my pre-college life, I suppose I struggled to be popular to a certain degree. Everyone wants, or even needs to be recognized sometimes. But it seemed that in my quest to become someone, there were certainly a lot of disappointments along the way. Many of my school friends found themselves at that long awaited point in their life, where they could be accepted into the "popular crowd". It was then that they seemed to change.

It hurt sometimes when those friends had to sacrifice their friendship with me in order to be "popular". I was different from the rest; I understood that.[15] It was only when I realized that I was *supposed* to be different that things began to change for the better. I

[15] 1 Peter 2:9

was a Mormon boy, and that certainly wasn't going to change. Once I realized that I only had to be what I was, everything seemed to fall into place. Soon, those around me began to accept me, just for me. My definition of "popular" was altered dramatically, not only for me but for everyone else as well.

Later on I realized that, although High School was pretty fun, it didn't really help me much in preparing for what would come next. Or perhaps, I missed the whole point of high school altogether. If I would have only known then what I eventually was to become later in life, I might have been a little more studious. In a lot of ways, my whole High School career can be boiled down to one crazy backflip; the backflip that collapsed every bit of solemnity at our graduation ceremony.

Marty was one of my best friends from school. He was a non-member, but he was as much a part of our group as any of us. We both had a deep interest in Drama. Not in any weird or geeky way. We didn't run around wearing make-up or anything, but the two of us always felt we could become performers of some sort. Marty sang with us and tried to learn any instrument he could get his hands on. He and I had a little standup comedy thing going on, and were often the life of the party around school. We especially liked to do crazy stunts. Often we could fool the teachers into believing that we were involved in a fist fight until they realized it was only us faking it.

I must mention that I was a pretty small kid, and still am I guess (at least on the inside). Marty, on the other hand, was about six foot three, weighing in at about two-hundred pounds. I believe he did play a little football, but his real love was music and acting. During these "fake fights", he would pick me up and hurl me about. I looked like the proverbial rag doll. But with practice, this flailing about became more and more controlled, even somewhat acrobatic. Eventually these moves evolved into a sort of flying back flip; with Marty throwing my feet up and over my head.

We were so proud of this great feat, that we felt it needed to be displayed before the whole student body. Well at least our graduating class. We spent days and days calculating the exact moment when we would pull this off. On the day before commencement practice, the principle manifestly informed the class that any "funny business" during graduation could result in losing our diplomas. We were sure that this only applied to legal stuff like public intoxication or indecency.

So there we were, sitting in our seats, about five rows back from the front. The group was split into two sides of the gym. As I remember it, each side consisted of about fifteen rows, each with about five people. The first one or two rows were set aside for honor students. Then it was our turn… the regular, ordinary students. We had decided that after I had received my diploma we would hand our caps and diplomas to another friend named Pat. And at that moment, we would perform our final act of total rebellion before the class, the faculty, and of course, the parents.

The pressure was building; our row was coming up soon. Just at the last possible moment, Marty declared that he couldn't go through with it. I desperately tried in vain to convince him to change his mind. I was so disappointed and mad that he, the veritable actor, would get cold feet right at the moment of truth. "Come on, Marty!" I yelled in a whisper. But he just turned and proceeded to the stage.

It seemed that all of this anticipation leading up to our great day of revolt had been utterly wasted. However, when I started down from the stage, I spied Marty slipping off his cap. Wasting no time, I quickly flung my cap and diploma cover like Frisbees. As planned, Marty launched me up, higher than ever. I hung in the air for what seemed like an eternity; coming down with a loud BOOM on the gym's hardwood floor. The entire room went wild, with the exception of the principle, of course. I looked up moments later and my mom and dad's mouths were still agape.

After repeated pats on the back as well as scowls from certain faculty members, Marty and I went to the local store to get supplies for our senior trip. The woman at the checkout looked at us and said, "You guys are the ones that did that flip thing aren't you?" I guess you could say that we had somewhat made our mark in that little town, if only for a moment.

Among other things, a new "non-denominational" Christian church had become pretty popular with many of the young people at school. It became apparent over time that this church focused much of its attention on the LDS Church. I recall many times when anti-Mormon literature would mysteriously find its way into my locker. Through our association, Marty had begun meeting with the missionaries in our ward. About that same time, he had also begun dating a girl who went to this other church; soon Marty became very confused as to why we were so hated by them.

I was thrilled at the prospect of my good friend Marty joining the Church. But he didn't get very far when his girlfriend gave him a certain book. The book was designed as an attempt to discredit the testimony and work of Joseph Smith. The confused Marty soon came to me saying that he could no longer meet with the missionaries, until he could "sort it all out". Nevertheless, he agreed to let me borrow the book so my dad and I could examine its contents. We of course found it to be full of many untruths and deception; taking quotes out of context, etc.

Needless to say, Marty halted his investigation of the Church. But we continued to stay close until I left for my mission, and a little bit after I returned. He even wrote me a couple of times. We have since found each other on Facebook and chat from time to time.

There is one important thing that I have

neglected to mention. It was during my High School years that all three of my older brothers left home for their missions. Paul and Perry, (the twins), were both called to go to Italy. They were gone during my tenth and eleventh years. Pat, the next brother, went to Thailand during my senior year. There is no question that I love all my brothers, I admit that. But for a number of various reasons throughout my young life the older two, Paul and Perry seemed to hang out together while Pat and I hung out with each other the most.

Growing up, Paul and Perry shared a room, while Pat and I were always roommates. Of course we all had many great times doing things together. But Pat and I had developed certain closeness on top of it all. I missed him terribly while he was in Thailand. My big brother Pat was the reason I didn't get initiated with a swirly in the boys' bathroom during my freshman year. I was always welcome whenever he would go off with his senior friends. We truly loved each other's company.

Before Pat left on his mission he pulled a fast one on me. He went and got himself a girlfriend. In those last few precious months before leaving, he spent all of his time with her. They even sort of promised to wait for each other before he left. Yet in the end, Pat had a change of heart in regards to his future while he was in Thailand. This made things somewhat difficult. She had been working very hard to make money for the both of them before his return. On top of that, she happened to be the sister of another close friend by the name of Steve.

If you asked me, I knew that it wouldn't work out from the very beginning. I just knew. It was really hard for Pat to focus on his mission before he left. I think he would agree with me even after all these years. It wasn't very smart to get a girlfriend so close to leaving. So I quickly put in my mind, "That will never happen to me!"

After High School, I started Junior College while Pat was away. All of my brothers had done the same before they left. In my usual lack of preparedness, I had only just started building my mission fund. I worked and worked, and then worked some more. After school I swept the floors and stocked the shelves at Wigwam, a local store. I built houses on the weekends with Brother Staley. Between classes, I worked for one of the Psychology instructors, Ms. Fouquette, who had a counseling practice on the side. I worked for her on and off campus grading tests and running errands. I also tutored other students. Psychology was one of my best subjects. Of course I had some incentive to try a little harder in that class, and her name was Heidi.

My first quarter at college was definitely an eye-opener. I learned early on that when exam time came around, it was a good idea to have studied for it. That was a new concept for me, given my experience in high school. I took a number of courses that year, but I will only elaborate on the Psychology class, which happened to be quite popular. Ms. Fouquette was a very dynamic instructor. Everyone liked her, and still do to my knowledge. Typical to my style, I always ended up sitting in the back of the room, usually next to a forty-something year old dad named Richard. For some reason, the class content came easy for me; but Richard seemed to struggle the whole time. As I did my best to help him, we soon became friends.

Each day in class, I would notice a particular girl who always sat at the front of the room. She had beautiful long black hair; which was all I saw of her because I barely made it to class on time, and was among the first to bolt out of the room at the end. I sometimes wondered what her face looked like, but for days I would forget to stick around long enough to see it.

It was only after we had our first test that I finally learned her name. Heidi had gotten the highest score. The teacher always spotlighted those students. She also put everyone's scores from top to bottom on the overhead projector, so we could see where each of us ranked in the class. This may have been some kind of Psychology experiment to analyze our reactions. To my surprise, my score was second from Heidi's top score. Of course I was pretty sure that my high score on that test was merely an anomaly.

Instinctively, my impression of Heidi, still not seeing her face, was that she must be some kind of nerdy bookworm who had nothing better to do than study for tests. In a short while, I found this perception to be far from the truth. With this realization, I must have expressed my interest in meeting her every day to Richard. So one day, he took it upon himself to invite her to come to lunch with us. Until that day I had never met a girl like her. To me she was everything, a four-point student, athletic, artistic, mature, funny, and of course, quite pretty. I know. I know. What happened to "That will never happen to me!"? I don't know what had come over me. I was falling into the same trap as my brother Pat!

Even though Heidi and I were the same age, she seemed so much more mature than I; and definitely way out of my league. Her agreeing to have lunch with me, I mean us, still boggles the mind. For the first time in my life I think I was a little bit shy.

At the cafeteria we all ate our lunch, carried on a pleasant conversation, and then Heidi left, with her boyfriend. I knew this guy. I had known him, or rather guys like him my entire life. "Mr. Popularity". He of course played basketball on the college team; you know the type. It figured that Heidi would be going out with someone like him. Nevertheless, for some reason, which I could never understand, our little lunch date became a fairly regular thing after class.

It wasn't too long before Heidi and I had become pretty good friends. I know it sounds terribly geeky, but we actually competed for the best scores in class.

Sometimes I could even beat her. I really started to like her. But just like clockwork, Mr. Popularity would always show up after lunch and ruin everything. Two months of this went by, and I was sure that our friendship would stay just that; which actually didn't bother me all that much with the mission being just around the corner.

A holiday dance was coming up at the college. As it was with High School, I rarely went to any of the school dances. There were always better ones at Church. Besides, this dance was a semi-formal dance that I had no intention of going to. Do you remember Pat, back at graduation? He held our stuff during that flip. Well, we both ended up at that same little local college. Pat would sometimes join our little lunch parties. In fact other friends eventually joined us as well.

In front of Heidi, Pat asked me whether or not I had found a date for the dance. I said that I wasn't really planning on going. "Why don't you take Heidi?" he asked. I was pretty sure she would be going with "you know who", so that's pretty much how I replied. Heidi's response was that she actually hadn't decided whom she would go with at that point. "Well then ask her!" Pat said. Knowing that she would likely be going with Mr. Popularity, I dismissively asked, "You wouldn't want to go with me, would you?" Nearly simultaneously, she began saying, "Why wouldn't I want to go with you? I think it would be fun." I tried to move on to another subject. But she persisted by clarifying that she really did want to go with me. I couldn't believe my ears. I was suddenly at a loss for words. To this day it still amazes me that she could see beyond my wimpy exterior and actually have any interest in me.

Don't forget that all this time, I really was preparing to go on my mission. I only had a few months till I would be turning nineteen. I suppose that I somewhat understood what my brother had gone through. Out of sheer weakness, I began dating her. Before I knew it, we were inseparable. In fact, we even took the same classes, just to be together.

As the weeks passed, Heidi and I found more and more things in common. We finally reached the point where I needed to tell her about my mission plans. She knew I was LDS, but I expected the same reaction from her that I always got from my non-member friends; they all thought the idea of a mission was crazy. But for some strange reason, Heidi seemed to understand. It was then that she revealed that she in fact was a Mormon herself. Actually, what she really said was that she "used to be one".

I learned that Heidi had stopped going to church only a short time before going away to college. I informed her that unless she was excommunicated, or had requested to have her records removed, she was still a member of the Church. It even turned out that her older brother had served a mission and was at the time living in Provo, Utah. I don't think she took me seriously until the time actually came for me to fill out, and send in my mission paperwork. To my surprise we actually argued about my going. She apparently didn't want me to go. I can honestly say that this became a very difficult predicament for me; something I had never expected.

I knew I had struck gold with Heidi. She was everything I ever wanted in a girlfriend, or so I thought. In a short time, she matter-of-factly announced that if I do leave for my mission, she would go off and join the Navy; the Navy? What was she trying to pull? I soon learned that she had already been thinking about this. She had clear aspirations for her education and career. With the military benefits, she felt that she could achieve her goals. I believe that her dad was a former Navy man, so it actually made sense after all.

I can see now how blessed I was to have one brother out in the mission field and two already home. I knew in my heart that I had a responsibility to everything that I believed in. As you already know, I went ahead and sent my papers in. My interview with Stake President Wilson went like clockwork. It just so happened that Brad, a good friend in the stake, was also submitting his papers. We both received our interviews about the same time; therefore, we expected that our calls would come around the same time as well.

In the midst of all that I was involved with, Heidi left school a quarter early. The next time I saw her, she had already joined the Navy. I won't lie; this whole breakup thing did hurt a little. While I was in the mission field, I got a letter from her telling me that she was already in officer's training. It had only been a few months. Yet I wasn't surprised because she had such a great aptitude for learning, among her other great qualities.

I recently checked up on Heidi via the internet and came to find out that she is still in the Navy; among a very elite group of women to become Captain and Commander; again, no surprises. As I write this, it is easy to see what a blessing the whole Heidi experience was. It would have been so easy to just give in and choose to be with her. Had that been my choice, all those years of planning and all the experiences I had on my mission could have been wiped away. In hindsight, it is really clear to me, particularly in light of what Elder Holland said, how much Satan was working on the both of us.[16] I also know now, that Heavenly Father was watching over me to help me reach my goals.[17]

[16] D&C 10:12
[17] Alma 37:37

Chapter 2: The Call

What a blessing it was to be able to attend the last quarter of school with my brother Pat. Now back from his mission, he began filling my head with many of his wonderful experiences in Thailand. He re-lived his mission for me over and over. More than ever, I was certain that I wanted to follow him and serve the Lord. He had many interesting stories about Thailand. The way he talked, mission life seemed relatively easy. They had a maid who would do all of their housework, and even cooked their meals. It didn't sound anything like the missionary life I had ever seen or heard about; I actually got a little taste of it before Pat came home.

Just before Pat returned, I had the opportunity to go out on splits with the elders in our ward. I had been inside their apartment a few times. It was small and not very clean. I knew they had to do their own laundry and cooking, etc. The first time we went out, I was paired up with an elder from some remote part of Utah. He was still fairly new in the field. I drove my truck to a small beach community across the island; all the while I was afraid that I might run into someone that I knew. Nevertheless, knowing that most of the people in this area were retirees, I thought I would be relatively safe.

I can recall times when Jehovah's

Witnesses would visit our house. They would always come in small groups. A couple of times, someone I knew from school would be amongst them. That was always a little awkward for the both of us; now I was finding myself on the other side. As we got out of the truck, I really didn't know what to expect.

We knocked on a few doors, finding no one home. Eventually, we managed to find a house where an elderly woman opened the door. The missionary commenced giving a somewhat lengthy introduction. The woman patiently waited for a pause, and then politely said that she wasn't interested. As she began to shut the door, the elder sneakily stuck his foot in the way to stop it. Holding the door open, he continued on with his message. I truly wanted to die. I thought, "If this is missionary work, I want no part of it".

My brother Pat on the other hand, had no stories like that one. He only had stories such as the time they found a young man to teach while playing basketball. I thought, "Now that's my kind of missionary work". It didn't take long to decide that Thailand was where I wanted to go. I seem to recall in the missionary application process, there was a place on a form where one can state a destination or a general area where you are interested to go. Of course I listed Thailand. I soon learned that what one might say in the application materials often has little to do with where he or she will end up going. Over the years, I have come to understand that the

Lord will send missionaries where He needs them. Some of the calls I have heard of seemed a perfect match, while others appeared very random.

Many things happened during that short time after Pat's return. But to my dismay, it didn't take long for Pat to find himself another girlfriend. In fact I helped him find her, and was there when they met.

I could see how much Pat loved Thailand and wanted to go back someday. After a little investigation, we learned that there were actually a few Thai people living in our area. Pat recalled that one was a girl who had worked at the same grocery store where he had worked before his mission. We further learned that she was still working there. I remember waiting in the car while they sat and talked during her entire lunch break. She was a really nice girl, and cute too. Her name was Bupar. She lived with her aunt, who was married to an American. Pat and Bupar quickly hit it off and began dating.

There I was, on the back burner once again. Thankfully, I still had my many friends to hang out with. That was one of the busiest summers that I can remember. We double dated, triple dated, and yes even quadruple dated. We sometimes went to church dances that were 2 or more hours away. We water skied and went bowling a lot too. Because I had already graduated, I was even allowed to chaperone at a 3 day stake youth conference. Technically I wasn't a youth anymore. In fact I had been an

Elder since I turned eighteen. Truthfully, chaperoning was actually just an excuse to hang out with my friends, who were still in the youth program.

I suppose that in the back of my mind, I was always thinking about my upcoming mission call. In the midst of the distraction of all the fun and games that summer, I scarcely realized that the day had crept up on me.

I had been out water skiing with my regular group of friends most of the day. Unusually, we finished early and found ourselves back at Steve's house. Despite the fact that my brother had recently broken up with his sister, Steve and I had become quite close over that year or so. We often just sat around and talked about a lot of things, but mostly… our missions.

Steve was also getting ready to go on his mission. He would go to college for a year like I did, except he planned on going to Ricks (BYU Idaho). Everybody knew that I could receive my call any day. All of my friends seemed as excited as I was about the impending call. I would be the first out of this little group to go.

Since we had come back early that day, we began talking about going out for pizza or something. But for no particular reason, I just felt like going home. That was very strange to everybody; because I was usually one of the main planners of what we did. I just didn't feel like going anywhere.

When I got home, seeing that no one was

there, I retrieved the mail from the mailbox. As you may have guessed, there was one particularly large and heavy envelope among the rest of the mail. And yes, it did have the Church logo on it. I didn't even have to open it to know what was inside, as it was addressed to me. My call had come, and I was at home… by myself. I knew I should probably have waited for the family to get home.

It is a tradition amongst many LDS families to have their son or daughter open their calls with everyone gathered around. So as I came through the door, I simply laid the envelope on the dining room table, and then wandered aimlessly around the house; perhaps I was trying to pretend that it hadn't really come. A couple of hours went by; I was still alone. I picked up that envelope over and over again. With nothing else to dwell upon, thoughts of countries and states reeled through my head.

Literally, where in the world would I be going? I thought of places my brothers and friends had gone. Paul and Perry went to Italy, Pat went to Thailand, Alan went to Spain, Jim went to California, and Jeff went to England. The other Jeff, one of my very best friends, was currently serving in Salt Lake City. I could go practically anywhere in the world; and all I had to do was open that blessed envelope.

Time continued to go by, as I gradually began to get frustrated. Where was everybody anyway? Why must I remain in this endless state of agony? Just then, a new thought leaked into my head, "What difference would it really make if I opened it right now?" As if acting on their own, my hands began ripping the top of the envelope. At that point, I realized that there was no turning back. It had to be revealed!

I pulled out the letter inside which read, "Dear Elder Morris you have been called to serve in the Japan, Fukuoka Mission (pronounced Foo-koo-oka). Japan? Japan? Why Japan? Incoherent thoughts were simultaneously racing through my head. I didn't know what to do first; nothing was coming to mind. I decided I should at least get on my knees and pray. With so many thoughts flying around in my head, I was having difficulty making any sense at all. Oddly enough, I did begin to feel a little calmer; so I planted myself on the couch to wait some more.

It didn't take long and my parents were home. Mom started to cry; and as he did when my brothers got their calls, Dad got out the big old, and outdated Atlas. It took me a little time, but eventually I located Japan on the map. After that, Dad pulled out some dusty old photos of his Navy days in Japan, back in the fifties. As soon as I arrived in Japan, I came to realize that those pictures had only given me a weird idea of what to expect there. Of course I was already pretty sure that everyday people weren't being pulled around in rickshaws anymore.

As soon as the family's accolades were

properly conveyed, I called Brad to see if he had gotten his call. He and I knew our calls would come about the same time, so we called each other often to check if anything had come. It turned out that his call had in fact come as well, and the same sort of commotion was happening over at his house. When the time came for us to share the details, without hesitation, I said, "You first".

I could hear Brad speaking, but in my own excitement I think I blocked out everything but the words "South Carolina". Go ahead, admit it. Deep down inside, don't most people feel that foreign missions are more exciting and challenging than going stateside? No offense intended, but aren't most people thinking that while they say something like, "the good people of (insert the stateside place) will get to hear the gospel from you, Elder"[18]. Of course, that just goes to show how little I understood about the way in which mission calls are extended.

I mentioned that my best friend Jeff had been called to the Salt Lake South mission almost a year before. When he called to tell me, I was a little uncomfortable as to how to react. I mean, "...what do you say to that?"[19] He and I had been quite the little radicals growing up in our tiny branch. Jeff's family moved there a couple of years after we did.

---

[18] Reference to a line from the film *The Singles Ward* (2002), Halestorm Entertainment

[19] Ibid.

Jeff and I had been buddies for the better part of nine years when he got his call. I don't know how we managed to survive some of the crazy things we did, and the pranks we pulled. There are so many of them to mention. Suffice it to say that thirty some years later, we might still get in trouble if people were to learn about some of the things that we did. That thought had actually crossed my mind. Maybe his call to Salt Lake was some sort of punishment for our shenanigans. I thought, "Really, who gets called to Salt Lake, the capital city of Mormonism?"

From where we sat in Washington State, what would missionaries have to do in Salt Lake? Where would the challenges be? But in reality, I later learned from Jeff that his mission had one of the highest baptism rates in the world. And I know that he had his fair share of challenges. Jeff and I still remain best friends, and if you asked him now, he would tell you that his mission was the greatest, life-changing decision he could have ever made. Of course I can say the same thing about mine as well. Today, more than ever I am convinced that the Lord sends his missionaries not only where they are needed most, but also where they need to go.

Nevertheless, once again that same uncomfortable feeling came when Brad said "South Carolina". I felt a twinge of guilt to tell him that I was going to far-off Japan. But when we both returned home, I realized that in a lot of ways, Brad's mission was almost as foreign as mine had been. I think I even detected a slight southern drawl when we both reported to Stake President Dickson.

If that name sounds familiar, President Dickson was the same Brother Dickson who served his mission to Mexico in the 60's. He had only just returned from being the president of the Mexico City North Mission when I left for the MTC. Not long after I left, he was called to lead our stake. In a few short years after that, President Dickson joined the Quorums of the Seventy, where he continues to faithfully serve the Lord. What a privilege it was to report to him, as he was such a wonderful role model to both Brad and me.

After I hung up the phone with Brad, I began calling all my other friends. I called everyone I could think of; I could hardly contain myself. Everyone was sincerely excited for me… telling me how great I will be. But as the dust settled, it started to dawn on me exactly what was about to happen. Truth be told, I think I felt a little scared.

There was a certain girl that I had gone out with from time to time. Her name was Cindy. Her dad was in the Stake presidency at that time, and yet he still let me go out with his daughter. In fact, I was pretty familiar with the whole family and would hang out at their house quite often. Shortly after I got my call, I went over for a visit. Coincidentally, it so happened that they had a Japanese exchange student staying with them for a few weeks. His name was Yasuyuki. I think he was about thirteen; his English was almost non-existent. Yet somehow, amongst all the well-wishing from Cindy's family, Yasuyuki was able to glean out the fact that I was headed for Fukuoka, Japan.

While Cindy's mom was pulling out a map, Yasuyuki kept saying, "Fukuoka? Fukuoka?" As the map unfolded he began perusing it with his finger. By his insistent gestures, we somehow managed to understand what he was trying to say. First he pointed to the city of Fukuoka, which was near the top of the island of Kyushu. He then slid his finger clear to the bottom of the island to the city of Kagoshima and said, "My home!" "My home!"

We figured that Yasuyuki was trying to say that his house was not far away from Fukuoka. But even I could see that the distance was very great. For all I knew, his house was in a completely different mission. Nevertheless, he gave me his home address to take with me. I very much enjoyed sharing what little bit of time Yasuyuki had before returning home to Japan. He even tried in vain to teach me a little Japanese; and I managed to show off what little Japanese I did know from a popular song of the day, "*Domo Arigato Mr. Roboto…*"[20]

Time quickly flew by, and I had only a few days before we were to leave for Provo. For my final date, I decided to take out a sweet girl named Pam who lived on the

[20] Reference to "Mr. Roboto", by the singing group Styx

neighboring island. Our Young Men's president, Brother Autry let me take his Corvette for the date. Once they received their calls, Brother Autry had a tradition of allowing some of the boys in the ward to go on their final date in one of his really nice cars. Mine was his 1967 Marina Blue Corvette. My brother Pat got to take out the 1923 T Bucket Roadster that we had built as a Young Men's project. As usual, I made this date with minimal forethought and planning.

That last date before leaving for my mission ended up just cruising around and eating at a Chinese restaurant. Nevertheless, it was an absolute blast. After I said goodnight to Pam, I found myself alone on a long straight stretch of road; there's a 390 horsepower engine under the hood; I knew I probably wouldn't find myself behind the wheel of a car until after my mission. Let's just say, it was all I could do to keep the car under a "reasonable" speed.

During all that was happening to me, Bupar had been taking the missionary lessons with Pat; it was exciting for me to witness a convert baptism so close to the start of my mission. I saw the joy that Pat felt knowing that his soon to be bride would be able to share the blessings of the gospel with him.

Pat and Bupar were married shortly before I was to leave for the MTC. For some reason, Pat asked me to be his best man at the wedding. He said that he couldn't think of anyone better for the job. That was a little hard for me to believe, but I really felt proud to be a part of that day. Pat would be going to BYU for the fall semester, so we would all be driving down to Provo together.

The drive from our house to Provo was 946 miles or so. We went a little early to help Pat and his new bride find a place to live. A few days after they had settled in, I would be saying goodbye to the world as I knew it… the beginning of a completely new life. Brad and I were set apart as missionaries for The Church of Jesus Christ of Latter-Day Saints on September 1 by Stake President Wilson. On September 8, we entered the Missionary Training Center in Provo, Utah.

On the trip down, my dad managed to put aside a little time for just the two of us to have a chat. He said that I would be leaving home as a boy and come back as a man… or something like that. I supposed that may have been what happened. Regardless, I cried as much like a baby when I had to come home as I did when I left.

At the MTC, our group would be the second and final orientation of the day. It was hard to say goodbye to everyone and go through that door; but somehow I managed. It was like nothing I had ever experienced before. I had never been separated from my family for such a long period. At the risk of sounding somewhat namby-pamby, I am not ashamed to say that I would sorely miss my mom and dad.

Today, mission costs are pro-rated, so that the cost of one mission is relatively the same as another. In those days, each mission had a different price tag. With two going at the same time, my brothers' missions to Italy were very expensive; I remember how my mom worked two jobs to make up for the extra costs. Pat's mission to Thailand was fairly inexpensive, and somewhat a relief to my parents. But my mission was going to be perhaps the most expensive. Nevertheless, my parents had decided early on that they would not ask for help in sending their boys out into the field. I learned during my mission that both my parents held down two jobs to make it all work.

During his little "becoming a man" speech, Dad made a promise that he would write to me every single week. While some were short and sweet, he was true to his word. Those letters, and the ones from my mom and grandma, proved to be a buoy for me throughout my whole mission. In those letters, I truly felt that I was not alone and in a way, I was sharing my mission with them. Dad was a new convert to the Church when he married Mom. Although he never served a mission, his insight, testimony, and support was invaluable to me all along the way. Also, being a convert, I know how Dad felt about the importance of the work. I will be forever grateful for my dad and the love and support that he and Mom provided for me.

My mind wandered as I sat with my family during the orientation at the MTC. Parents and their missionaries were soon exchanging tearful hugs. We were then escorted towards a certain doorway. Saying goodbye was somewhat painful, yet at the same time, my heart was racing with excitement.

Chapter 3: The MTC

The first thing I remember when I went through the door was coming upon a table, behind which an elderly sister was seated. We were to drop off our paperwork and then pick up a packet. When I handed my papers to the sister, she scanned for my name on a roster and then with a puzzled look said, "Elder Morris, you have already come through here." I told her that this was the first time for me.

The kind sister then clarified with me that my name was in fact Peter Morris, and that I was in fact going to Japan. I answered both questions in the affirmative. "Sendai, Japan?" she asked, "No, Fukuoka." I replied. She deduced that there must have been another Elder Peter Morris who had taken my packet by mistake. She located and gave me his packet, and I moved along with the other elders. Later that evening I managed to exchange packets with my Peter Morris counterpart and everything was back in order. What are the odds of that ever happening, really?

Each dorm room had two sets of bunk-beds for four elders. This place I shall never, ever forget. Elder Frandson from Utah and Elder Thomas from Nebraska made up one pair. My companion was Elder Stoneman. He looked to be about 220 pounds and probably six foot four. Elder Stoneman was a laid back, slow talking boy from Spanish Fork, Utah. I didn't know much about the towns in Utah, but I knew there was something different about his. He spoke with a distinct drawl.

We learned that Stoneman had been going to BYU on a scholarship. By his slow manner of speech and athletic physique, I naturally assumed his scholarship was a football or basketball scholarship. To be honest, my first impression of him was that he was not one of the brightest people I would meet at the MTC. That just shows you how one should not judge the proverbial book by its cover. "A football scholarship?" I asked. "Nope, academic" he replied. Truth be told, Elder Stoneman turned out to be one of the smartest people I have had the privilege of knowing to this day. He actually reminded me a little of my dad.

Stoneman and I quickly developed a special friendship. I wonder if he realizes just how much he meant to me throughout my entire mission. Although it was usual practice to call each other by the title "Elder", we tended to be more on a first name basis. We came to know each other inside and out. I learned about his family. He often expressed how much he loved his family, and the Gospel. He had a lot of love. I consider myself fortunate that he shared some of his with me.

After getting acquainted with each other, we were told that we would be having dinner and then go straight to our first Japanese class. I thought, "Gosh! They don't waste any time at all do they!?" We didn't even have a chance to settle in. I soon learned the urgency of what we were about to embark on;

those eight weeks turned out to be excruciatingly short.

Our first language class was absolutely unforgettable. We had two wonderful teachers. First was a soft spoken young man by the name of Elder Campbell. The other, Elder Ratelle, was a stout young man who possessed a somewhat bolder presence. While both seemed to have contrasting characters, they shared the same kind of love for what they were doing. In that first class, not a single word of English was spoken, but somehow we managed to glean a little from what they were trying to say to us. At one point during the class, it became clear that they were bearing their testimonies. Suddenly the spirit changed, as did the expressions on their faces.

After an hour or so, we learned how to introduce ourselves in Japanese. We continued with that for the rest of the class. When class was over, we understood why this was so important. Our schedule showed that following class, we would be having a branch meeting.

Each branch was set up according to where the missionaries would be going. I don't think I will ever be able to erase that night's meeting from my memory. Each week, when a new group of elders joined the new branch, they were required to stand and *try* to give a self-introduction in Japanese. I really wish I would have paid better attention during that first class.

At my farewell, I had been given one of those "Missionary Journal(s)". You probably know these, a bound book complete with "before and after" picture boxes at the front. There was a page for every day. Almost everyone I knew had one. I never wrote a single day's worth of Journal in it. I only wrote the date of the first day on the first journal entry page, but was too exhausted to write anymore.

I did however happen to have with me a year-long, pocket-sized day planner. On that first day, I simply jotted down the particulars of the day. Ironically, that practice continued, going through two more planners until the end of my mission. Every day is chronicled in detail. From this point forward, I will be extracting some of the details from these, along with letters that my parents saved for me; if I can interpret my own writing.

Perhaps I should introduce the rest of our MTC group. It won't be hard to figure out who excelled above the others. I already mentioned my roommates. What I forgot to mention was that Elder Stoneman's older brother had also served a mission to Japan. Lucky for him, Stoneman managed to get a little jump start before this first day. Not only him, but one of the others in the group, Elder Brinley had taken some Japanese in college before coming. This put Stoneman and Brinley at an advantage. Not an unfair advantage, but an advantage none the less.

Elder Dechman was Brinley's companion or "dode" as we called them later, which is short for "doryou", meaning companion. The last two in the group were Elder Dallimore and Elder Wright. I must admit that the Japanese class was somewhat difficult for me. After eight weeks, I am sure I was at or near the bottom of the group when it came to comprehending the language and the lessons.

Even after a year of college, I realized that I had come to the MTC fully unprepared. The routine was eye opening, literally. Prying my eyes open every morning at six A.M. was an extremely difficult task for me. I don't know why this was so; I got up much earlier than that to do chores and attend early morning Seminary all through high school. Perhaps it was because the first class of the day was Gym. I can tell you in honesty that I wasn't too awfully vigilant about getting up that early to do push-ups and sit-ups.

But when I did go to the gym, I sure did enjoy the volleyball and basketball. It was a great opportunity to get out some of the frustration from class. In relation to that, I noticed that there were an extraordinarily high number of elders on crutches at the MTC. I think that two of my brothers also ended up on crutches while they were there. I guess it's just something about a couple of thousand nineteen-year-old boys and competitive sports.

After gym, we showered up and went to breakfast. I couldn't understand all the complaining about the food at the MTC. I don't remember ever complaining, but others seemed so spoiled and nit-picky about the so-called "lousy food". I can only speak for myself, but

I can't tell you how much I missed that cafeteria line when I finally got to Japan.

This is actually my first letter home:

Dear Mamasan & Papasan:

Well here I am at the MTC. Ooooweee! It's hard! We have about 10~11 hours of class and study… My companion's name is Elder Stoneman. He is the biggest Choro (Elder) in the District (The Fukuoka District). Tomorrow they pick our DL; I hope it's not me. I seem to be getting some of the language, it's pretty fun, but TIRING. I hope I don't fall behind. The first day, we had a branch meeting after our first language class. There are 8 of us and we were all embarrassed when they had us stand in front and tell them (in Japanese) where we were from and who we are… Especially when we would finish with "Yoroshiku Onegaishimas" (Please accept us). Then they yell back the same and go "Oooooo!" high or low depending on how well you do it. Most of us did pretty good. If you can find my patriarchal blessing, I need it for support.

Sacrament meeting was just great. The whole meeting was in NIHONGO (Japanese) …Amazingly enough, I could understand a lot of it. I want to learn a lot but it's sometimes a little discouraging. I need a lot of encouragement…. I've got to get studying before I get behind. I mainly wrote to give you my address. Take care! Domo Arigato!

Love, Pete

Dear Pete,

Don't faint, I told you I'd write every week so why are you so surprised? We received your first letter and I'm glad to hear that you're not being overwhelmed by all the study. There is absolutely no doubt in my mind that you can master the language and the discussions without a lot of trouble. It sounds like you've also got a companion who has his head screwed on right too. I think it's good that he's a big guy, now there's one that's big on the outside and one who's big on the inside, and that should make a pretty good combination. I'm looking forward to each of your letters and I'm praying that each one will tell us of your continuing success.
Well it's back to work again, and it's still as much of a drag as usual. I really don't like working, I'd

rather play but I've grown accustomed to eating. I guess I have to keep on working.

Well Elder Petey, lunch time is over so I'll have to sign off for now. If I hurry I can get Mom to mail this thing when she goes out at her lunchtime. We all love you son and as always pray for your health and success. I've searched the house from top to bottom and can't find your Patriarchal Blessing. I'll contact the Stake and see if I can get a duplicate. Just for fun, go through all your stuff again. Till next week.

Love, Dad

Following breakfast, we were off to the first class of the day. We had about three hours of class before lunch and another three until dinner. That night, we studied as a branch for another couple of hours. This was a chance to mingle with other Japan missionaries who were in various stages at the MTC. This was also an opportunity to pass off our discussions with fellow missionaries. Before you leave the MTC, your goal was to pass off all of the eight discussions, three times. It is set up quite a bit different now, but that was the way that we did it. I shouldn't have been surprised at my extremely weak memorization skills, since I all but gave up on scripture mastery in Seminary.

I struggled and struggled; but it didn't take long for me to realize how normal my lack of ability was. I can recall a few missionaries that had a rougher time than I did. Over the ensuing weeks in Provo, one gets more familiar with some elders over others. I had befriended a young man who had several obstacles that, in my opinion caused him to toil a little more than others. I don't mean that he had any kind of learning disabilities or anything; but he did bring with him some distracting baggage.

My new elder friend had been in the BYU marching band before coming up to the MTC. Apparently, he was quite talented. Here we were in the MTC through September and October, the height of football season. Those familiar with the location of the MTC know that it is just up the hill from the Y's football stadium. Saturday (game day) was our Preparation Day (P-day). As we wrote our letters, we could hear the cheering from our dorm; our windows faced directly toward the stadium. If it weren't for away-games, that elder might have gone completely crazy.

It seemed that my good friend had yet another distraction that clearly kept his mind off the work. I was a little disappointed when I found out that he wasn't the only missionary with such a distraction. I'm sure that by now they have found a way to fix this problem, but it turned out that unofficial visiting hours had been established at the MTC. The grounds were bordered by chain-linked fencing that created a zoo-like setting for those on the outside. Many missionaries had visitors meet them in the evening hours along the fence. Sometimes they were buddies from the Y bringing pizza, but more often than not, they were girlfriends.

I doubt that there was anything more than just talking at that fence; but if I had been one of those being visited, I can only imagine how hard it would have been to concentrate on anything else. I truly felt sorry for this new friend of mine. One evening, when all the elders were sleeping, something woke me so I got up to visit the bathroom. Coming back I heard whispering in the stairwell. As I approached, I found that same elder anguishing in tears over his lesson book. "Dude, what's going on" I asked. "I just can't get it…" he replied.

Over the next hour or so, crouched on one of the steps, he and I endeavored to memorize and pass off that lesson. We then sat and visited for a while. I told him my opinion of what I believed was holding him back. It wasn't long until he too realized the distraction and got rid of it. We kept in touch during our missions, in spite of the fact that he went elsewhere in Japan.

I also saw my friend Brad a couple of times during his short two weeks there. We were able to see each other on the Sunday before he left for South Carolina. We didn't talk much, but I was already missing him. I got up very early to see him off the following morning. I didn't bother to wake up Stoneman, and was back before the alarm clocks went off.

Speaking of alarms; in the envelope that my call came in, there was also a list of items to bring with us to the MTC. They tell you to bring so many white shirts, so many sets of underwear, miscellaneous toiletries; and what turned out to be a real menace, an alarm clock. I'm sure that nearly everyone who receives that letter goes out with Mom or Dad and labors over what kind of clock to buy. I was amazed to find that there were so many different types of alarm clocks at the MTC. I saw and heard itsy bitsy beeping clocks, some with a large brass bell on top, and some with two bells. There were buzzing and chiming clocks as well. Some were equipped with a snooze feature that allowed a replay of the original sound every five minutes.

The first morning in our room was memorable to say the least. Everybody had set their alarms to go off at 5:30, but nobody thought to synchronize the clocks the night before. One of the elders' clocks had a very loud bell that went off first, followed by another with a beeping sound, and finally a second round of bells. I don't even remember if my alarm ever even went off. After a couple of mornings of that, one of us called a desperately needed room meeting, where we decided to take turns with the alarm clocks. What a blessing that was.

Dear Dad,

It's my first full P-Day today, BANZAI! We slept in too late to go to the temple though, but we'll go twice next week. I washed some clothes and wrote some friends. Then we went to the mall. I just got back. BYU just scored again, I can hear the crowd through this window. Anyway thanks for writing, I was beginning to give up hope. I don't like it here… but it's great! My brain seems to be swelling because it hurts so much. Too much frustration I guess. The guys here are crazy… wild and crazy. They get a kick out of turning all showers on hot and sit around in the shower room like it was a steam room.
It feels great not being an "atarashii senkyoshi" (new missionary). Everyone is getting ready to go to dinner and I have to get dressed. When I talk to other elders whose parents aren't members, I feel blessed to know that my parents understand what's going on. Dad, I love you and you are in my prayers every single time I pray. Please tell Mom that I love her too and miss her.

Your little son,   Pete

Dear Pete,

We received your last letter yesterday and both Mom and I had to read it over again to believe it was from you. The words on the paper didn't compute with the kid we left in Utah. Seriously, I'm really happy to hear that you are beginning to understand the Lord's ways and how he is restricted by his own rules from coming to our aid until we ask. It seems very difficult for people to grasp this principle but it's really true. Keep on praying for us because we really need it.

You remember of course the futile search for your Patriarchal Blessing and how we turned the house upside down trying to find it. Anyway last Sunday morning on the way to church I looked down and in one of the pockets in the van was a white envelope. Now I know that envelope wasn't there before. Anyway I pulled out the envelope and in it was your Patriarchal blessing in the envelope Patriarch Dickson sent it in. I believe that was there because Mom and I prayed for it to be found.
I'm beginning to feel that you are starting to get to know our Heavenly

Father and his Son. You can feel the love They have for us. That love is not too different than the love earthly parents feel for their children.

Well son lunchtime is over I've got to go. We love you, always. Keep working hard and be proud to be who you are and what you stand for.

Love, Dad

Our P-days were greatly anticipated each week. Along with the clean sheets, P-day was a great day all together. On those days we were able to go to a morning session or two at the Provo Temple on the hill. I had only been once to the newly opened Seattle Temple. I very much enjoyed the spirit there. My wife and I truly enjoy going to the temple as often as possible. It wasn't until I was sealed to her that I fully understood what is taught there. What a blessing the temple is in our lives.

We could also go down to the BYU campus on P-Day. We would get our hair cut at the Wilkinson Center or grab a bite at the Cougar Eat. Sometimes we took the bus and went to the mall. That was great, but I do think it took me a little extra time to get my mind back in the game at the MTC. That's probably why they don't allow missionaries outside the MTC anymore.

There is one particular P-Day activity that my companion and I rather enjoyed. While technically it may have been against the rules, it was one memory that I will never forget. By this time, my good friend Steve had started college up at Ricks (now BYU Idaho). He had been planning a trip to come down and see me. We agreed that P-day would be the best day to meet, so we could have lunch or something. I had done that with Jeff just before my going into the MTC. Remember, he was serving in Salt Lake at the same time.

Steve not only came down to Provo, but it turns out he had procured some tickets to that afternoon's football game. How could we pass that up? This may date me a little, but Steve Young was the quarterback in that game. How great was that? But time flew by and we had to leave early from the game to make it for dinner. We really enjoyed that P-day. Thanks Steve.

Sundays also turned out to be a highlight of our stay at the MTC. Our Sunday School class reminded me of a class at a youth conference, or maybe what one might experience at EFY. It was very fulfilling and well worth the time. Our teacher, Brother Wilcox was wonderful. He had such a sweet spirit about him. I can hardly remember his lessons as far as content was concerned, but my heart was pierced every week. Brother Wilcox ended each lesson with a song. Sometimes it was a variation of a hymn. But more often than not, he would favor us with a song that he had composed himself.

Brother Wilcox's songs were a form of

his testimony that rang out loud and clear. Because of him, my strength of testimony was raised several notches. He called on us to take Moroni's challenge in the Book of Mormon:

> And when ye shall receive these things, I would exhort you that ye would ask God, the Eternal Father, in the name of Christ, if these things are not true; and if ye shall ask with a sincere heart, with real intent, having faith in Christ, he will manifest the truth of it unto you, by the power of the Holy Ghost.[21]

By meeting this challenge, I found that many of the Gospel teachings soon came to my recollection quite fluidly. I often tried to find time alone to ponder upon those things. My relationship with my Heavenly Father and Savior began to grow from that point forward. With some of the members from his musical group, Brother Wilcox put on a little concert for us near the end of our stay there. He was also very kind to give us a tape recording of his songs. Even today, although I no longer have the tape, some of those songs remain inside my head.

This routine continued in much the same way for the rest of my time at the MTC. Day in and day out, we learned and grew. But once in a while, things would happen which would break

[21] Moroni 10: 4

up the monotony. There was a sister from Japan, who was preparing to go back home as a missionary. She had been going to school in the States, and was thus permitted to make her preparations in Provo. Today, everyone from Japan goes to Provo.

Something special happened with that sweet sister that has stuck with me, even to this day. One day she and an elder, also from Japan, were in the hallway singing a song to the tune of "The Farmer in the Dell". Except the words that they sang in Japanese were "Nihon ni kaeritai, nihon ni kaeritai… ōkii hikouki de, nihon ni kaeritai…" which means "I want to go back to Japan, I want to go back to Japan… on a big airplane, I want to go back to Japan." I hadn't been at the MTC long enough to understand all the words, so I asked her what it meant.

Instead of simply translating the words, this wonderful sister began to tell me why she sang it. She started by telling me that she was the only member in her family. She then bore her testimony of the joy that she had felt when she became a member; now she would have the chance to share that joy with her own people of Japan. The tears gradually welled up in her eyes; they pooled up in mine too, as she told me how much she loved her family and wanted that same joy for them one day. Although she loved being in Utah, and around so many faithful members, Japan was where her heart was. Her message continued to resonate in my mind during the remaining weeks. I am quite sure it helped me prepare for where I was going, and what I was about to do.

Another treasured memory, which I shall never forget happened at a weekly devotional. Each week, we had the opportunity to meet as elders and sisters of the MTC. At these devotionals, we often heard from our general authorities who would grace us with a motivating talk. I can still go back to notes that I took and remember how special they were. Early on, I learned that the MTC had a missionary choir which would sing at these meetings. I soon joined it. It was fun to sing with so many talented missionaries.

At one of the devotionals, our guest was Elder David B. Haight. At that point, I only had one experience meeting an apostle before. That was when Elder Bruce R. McConkie came to split our stake, shortly before I left for Provo. I can still recall how big his hand was to me when I shook it. Elder Haight and his wife both gave wonderful talks. Sister Haight spoke on obedience, and then Elder Haight spoke about feeling the spirit. He quoted Winston Churchill, "Men occasionally stumble over the truth; but most of the time, pick themselves up and hurry on as if nothing happened". This quote rang true to me as I would soon endeavor to spread the truth in Japan.

Elder Haight continued to say that we should have the power and influence such that those we teach will believe us. The power of this apostle's words caused my heart to swell.

[22] His talk inspired me so much that I really wanted to thank him personally. The only problem was that the congregation was asked to remain seated until he and his wife had left the room. Lucky for me, sitting in the choir behind the stand, I managed to slip out through the door behind the risers.

From the back door, I ran around the building to the front entrance. Seeing that there was no one there, I assumed that I was too late, and that Elder Haight had already left. Another elder with the same intent showed up behind me. I told him that we probably missed him. Just then, we heard voices coming from down the hall. Suddenly I got cold feet, but there was nowhere to flee except back out the front door. He saw us standing there, walked directly toward us, and stopped to shake our hands. We proceeded to tell him how much we enjoyed his talk.

Elder Haight looked down the hall and said, "There must be an empty room nearby, why don't we sit and talk…" With his arm around my shoulder, he opened a door to an empty office and then sat down at the desk there. We sat across from him for what must have been only a minute or two, but it seemed much longer. He told us how proud he was of us for our service, and then continued with an assurance that we would both be great missionaries. I could really feel his sincere love. I was instantaneously pumped up and revitalized.

[22] From personal notes: October 18, 1983

The MTC was the beginning of the creation of a new identity for me. I could feel a clearly defined changing process taking place. It was so hard to say goodbye to my friends and all that was familiar to me back home. I was pretty sure that nothing would ever be the same when I got back. Sure, it was scary but at the same time it was the most exciting thing that I had ever done.

I was making new friends, experiencing new things, and feeling new feelings. Soon, I would be traveling the furthest from home that I had ever been. I didn't realize it at the time, but I had been able to absorb more knowledge in those short eight weeks than at any other time in my life. You may find this hard to believe, but some nights I even dreamt in Japanese. After a day of learning how to pray in Japanese, my companion told me that I had said some of the words in my sleep. I guess I was as ready as I would ever be; next stop, Japan.

Chapter 4: Sayonara Life

The evening before we were to leave, everyone was allowed to call home one last time. I had hoped that our flight plan would include a stop in Seattle. Pat's trip to Thailand worked out such that we were able to drive down to say our final goodbyes to him in person. I was somewhat disappointed to learn that we would be going through San Francisco rather than Seattle. So I had to resort to saying my goodbyes over the phone, which was very difficult. The long distance hugs that we exchanged didn't quite have the same effect; yet the tears running down my face confirmed just how much I loved my mom and dad. I was going to miss them very much.

The following morning, at two o'clock, we faced our day of reckoning with excited minds, and dragging bodies. Our plane was scheduled to leave from Salt Lake International Airport at five-thirty. Most of us still had some last minute packing to do. We were to clean up any evidence of our stay and get our dirty sheets down the laundry chute.

At last, we checked in at the lobby for a final inspection and to receive our itineraries, passports, and plane tickets. The bus for the airport was already waiting out front. We were joined by an additional two sisters, who were also heading for the Fukuoka Mission. We didn't know them very well, because they had been in a different group and branch this whole time.

I suppose that I was still feeling a little down about not seeing my family at the airport; I knew that most of the other elders would be hugging and kissing theirs when we arrive. I hadn't got the final word on it, but Pat had said that he and Bupar would try to come to see me off. If he did come, he would have to be the designated well-wisher of the family. Today, due to airport security, families are not able to do this; but when we arrived at the airport we were greeted by a myriad of balloons and signs.

The ecstatic families rushed toward their missionaries with arms wide open. I was the only one there with no party to greet me. Even the elders from out of state had friends from BYU. My dear brother Pat wasn't to be found. So I think that out of pity, some of the elders were kind enough to share their families with me. Elder Stoneman's parents were especially kind to make me feel at home. By the way they surrounded him, I could see how proud they were of their son.

The time to board the plane came and everyone else began to say their final goodbyes. I had all but given up hope, when Pat and Bupar suddenly appeared on the escalator. I was so happy to see familiar faces. Pat and I hugged until the final boarding was underway. It was very hard to say goodbye. My last link to the world as I knew it was now being torn away from me. I was on my own, sort of. I took one final glance and a quick wave to my brother, and there would be no turning back.

This happened to be my very first jet plane ride; I did have a chance to go up in Steve's dad's Cessna a summer or two before. That was pretty fun, but the lift on this plane was so much more amazing; better than the Hammerhead ride at the county fair back home. The flight seemed very brief, as we soon began our descent into San Francisco International. We would make our first flight change and then it was on to the next leg, Tokyo. Salt Lake to Tokyo was 5,708 miles or so. I think that we were all excited, knowing that the next time we would set foot on the ground, it would be on Japanese soil.

I believe it was at this point that I began to have doubts as to whether or not I was up to this missionary thing. But it wasn't so much the language that I feared. Sitting there on that plane, I think I began wondering if I could even cut it as a missionary. What if nobody wanted to take what I had to offer? What if all I got was rejection? What if…?

As we settled into our seats on that 747, there was a little small-talk amongst us, and then everyone became quiet. We were looking a ten hour flight ahead of us. After the seatbelt light went off, most of the others went right to sleep. I couldn't even close my eyes for all the excitement. My seat happened to be located on the aisle side of an inside row. After a couple of hours, I noticed something curious. About four rows ahead, and to my right, I detected a pair of sparkling brown eyes peering over the seat. For several minutes, they continued to appear and disappear.

I must have been the only one in our group to notice that we were being spied upon. I waived my hand a couple of times with no response. At last, tiny finger tips began to wiggle above the top of the seat. As I waived again, a head slowly emerged above the seatback. It was an adorable little girl about eight years old. With our plane headed for Japan, I felt that it was safe to assume that she was Japanese; so I motioned for her to come over. At first, she bashfully shook her head "no". I tried again. This time, she carefully moved into the isle, and little by little made her way towards the side of my seat. A wave of terror now came over me. I thought to myself, "Good job; now you've done it; what on earth are you going to say?"

When she finally did reach my seat, I blurted out the only thing I could think of, in my infantile Japanese. "Konnichi wa, watakushi no namae wa Morris Choro desu." Translation: "Hello, my name is Elder Morris". I thought I had said it pretty well. But she made sort of a strange look, giggled, and scampered back to her seat. I couldn't make out what they were saying, but when she reported to her mother what had just taken place they were both laughing at my expense, or so I assumed. Although slightly embarrassed,

I realized that I had just spoken Japanese to my first real Japanese person outside of the MTC.

With my new found confidence, I decided to give it another try and motioned for the little girl to come back again. As before, she slinked her way back to my seat, where I then said, "Anata no namae wa nan desu ka?" *What's your name?* She giggled yet again; but this time she didn't go back. Instead she looked straight into my eyes and said, "I can speak English you know…" If I had closed my eyes, I could have sworn that she was an ordinary little American girl. "You speak English?" I asked. She nodded her head up and down. I continued, "Okay, what's your name then?" She smiled a big partially toothless grin and said, "Chihiro, what's yours?"

The little girl's name was Chihiro Nakazawa. She was on her way back to Sendai Japan with her mother and little brother. She went on to tell me that they were visiting her Grandmother who was living in Canada. She also happened to attend an international school where they learn in both English and Japanese. For the rest of the flight, little Chihiro toggled between her seat and mine. We talked and talked. She taught me a lot of new Japanese words and even how to write a few things. She also acted as a translator between her mother and me. They asked me a number of questions about me, and about my family. I even showed her pictures of my dog, King.

Chihiro and I enjoyed each other's

company very much during what seemed a very short six or seven hours. That little girl did more for me than I think she could ever realize. Thanks to her, my missionary experience got a wonderful jump start. Yet sadness began to overshadow the mood when we neared Tokyo, realizing that we would have to part ways.

In vain, I tried to fight the choked up feeling in my throat when little Chihiro began to cry. I didn't understand most of what her teary-eyed mother was saying; nevertheless, I could feel of her love as she said goodbye to me. In a very short time, it seemed that we had become very close friends. It was on that flight where I first came to understand the kind of spiritual influence that missionaries can have on others… if they just try.

Finally we were on our last leg of the trip; the remaining 586 miles that would complete my 7,240 mile journey from our house in Washington to Fukuoka, Japan. We had been traveling between twelve and thirteen hours already; all ten of us were extremely exhausted. As soon as the plane took off, I was out like a light. In what seemed only an instant, we were already about to land. Had I known then what landing would mean for me; I might not have gotten off that plane. From here on out I was looking at countless hours of study, endless miles of walking or riding bicycles, hundreds upon hundreds of doors to knock upon, spiritual low points, and rejection. You know, it's funny that I can hardly remember most of those difficult times.

Here we are; Japan, a whole new world. For months, everything I saw or did was a brand new experience. Over the years, I have enjoyed watching my five little babies grow and develop. I have loved watching the looks on their faces as they discovered that they could stand up, take a step alone, or clap their hands together. That was me stepping off that plane. I was a new born baby missionary; each day discovering my new found abilities.

Aside from the fact that one of my suitcases was lost in transit, and I would be without half of my wardrobe for several days, we successfully made it to Fukuoka. As we came down the escalator, we saw our little welcoming party. I'll never forget President Shimizu's Teddy-Bear face smiling up at us. As we reached the bottom, he called us each by name and then hugged us, one by one. Through that one brief squeeze, I could feel the genuine love and concern he had for me.

President Shimizu was going to be our dad in Japan for the duration of our stay. His lovely wife, Sister Shimizu was wonderful as well. She had previously been a nurse, which was helpful on many occasions. I can recall a few times when she actually seemed to take on the role of a mom to me. Now assembled, we loaded up in a couple of vans and made our way to the "Hombu" or mission home. It was pretty late, so we were sent straight to bed. Overcome with jetlag, we were allowed to sleep into the late morning.

After breakfast, the Hombu staff officially introduced themselves with a small orientation. Then we went downtown by bus. This would be my first ride on a public bus. As I looked out the window, I can still remember the newness and sense of wonder of being in such a foreign place. The only other times I had left the United States was through the north and south borders. This was nothing like that.

Our first stop was at the city office to get ourselves registered as foreigners or "gaijin". As such, each time we moved to another city, we were required to register with that city office. Next, we went to the bank to exchange our dollars into yen and open a new account. That day, everything that we did was a new and wonderful adventure. Afterward, the elders took us on a tour around the city by bus.

That evening we would get our first chance to proselytize in Japan. To be honest, I was absolutely terrified. Each of us would be paired up with an elder from the Hombu; a couple of us were even able to go with Japanese elders. Upon our return, each of us had a different experience to share.

I was able to go with Elder McIntire, the Hombu secretary. He took me out to do some house to house, after giving me a few pointers as to what to say at the door. I could feel the little muscles just under my skin twitching. I was truly frightened. Upon leaving, McIntire handed me a piece of paper with some appropriate words to use at the door approach. If a woman opened the door, I was to ask if her husband was home. We used the honorific word for husband, "go-shujin". The word "shu" means Lord; I recognized that from the MTC. Repeatedly, we used the term "Shu Iesu Kurisuto" or The Lord Jesus Christ. Using it so much I am sure that phrase was infused into my brain.

I watched Elder McIntire knock on a couple of doors, and then it was my turn. Fortunately for me, my first door was a woman; I was able to repeat the line that I had been rehearsing. While asking if her husband was home, it turned out that I had actually asked if the Lord Jesus Christ was home that night. The puzzled look on her face and lack of response told me that I didn't get it right. Nevertheless, with McIntire's help, it turned out to be just the right missionary question anyway. It was probably out of pity for me that she invited us in. As a result, we found our way back to the Hombu with a newly acquired bag of mandarin oranges.

When we all had made it back, we each related our brand new proselytizing stories. One in our group had gone out with an AP or Assistant to the President, who would be heading home the next day. I may not have the story exactly right, but I believe that in the story, the AP took the "Green Bean" to a high point in the city. Without explaining what he was doing, he turned towards the city lights below, raised his arms above his head; and like Samuel the Lamanite[23], began screaming. I suppose that the words he said must have been something like "Fukuoka no minasan, KUIARATAMENASAI!" which, loosely translated means "People of Fukuoka, REPENT!"[24] Later, the AP related to us that he had wanted to do that his whole mission… or something to that effect.

The following day we had our interviews, followed by a little testimony meeting, where we would also learn who our first companion or trainer was going to be. Some of them had even come to the Hombu to escort us to our first area. During that day, other elders who had reached the end of their missions began to gather at the Hombu. They had their exit interviews with the "Buch" (BOOCH), which was short for DENDO BUCHO or Mission President.

I'll try my best to put in order all the details. We began the testimony meeting with each of the APs speaking. Then some of the returning missionaries bore their testimonies. It was obvious that each one seemed very sad to go home. There was one particular elder that lost some of his composure when he stood up. As he struggled to speak, he shared with us that he had not been able to baptize a single person. Without saying as much, it seemed that he felt that his time there was an utter waste. He continued on by telling us that he had certainly grown spiritually, but continued to emphasize the point that all of

---

[23] Helaman 13: 4
[24] D&C 34:6

his hard work had yielded no fruit. By the looks on the faces of the others in his group, I don't think he was alone.

Listening to that elder, I felt a sense of anxiety at the prospect of my replacing these seemingly good and hardworking elders. Yet part of me was saying, "That isn't going to be me when I leave this place!" I soon came to understand very quickly that this wasn't going to be easy; over the next few days I would come to this eye opening realization.

The Buch gave us all some words of encouragement, and then bore his testimony. Following his remarks, each of us greenies were given our assigned area and companion. I don't remember where most of the others went, but Dallimore and I were going to Kagoshima. My new companion was Elder Jeffery from Delta, Utah. He was short like me, with rusty blonde hair and glasses. My good friend Stoneman was off to a place called Naze, located on a remote island. It seemed a very fitting name because in the MTC we had learned that the word NAZE meant 'WHY" in Japanese. Later I found out that the two words were merely homonyms. There was one consolation to our parting though. Stoneman and I would be in the same zone. That sounded great, except for the fact that from Kagoshima, Naze was about twelve hours by boat.

The thought of being apart from Stoneman made me a little sad, but I had other things weighing on my mind that kept me plenty busy. The next morning we rode about five and a half hours on a train. This was to be my first train ride. In two days' time I had several "firsts"; the plane, the bus, and now the train. It must really seem as though I was some sort of hick from the sticks. Jeffery and I joined Elder Rollings, who was replacing a Zone Leader or ZL in Kagoshima. The three of us would be going to the same area.

Dallimore met his companion at the EKI (train station) when we arrived. From the eki, the three of us took a taxi to our apartment. Actually, it was a small house. To our surprise, or perhaps our dismay, no one was home. Apparently Elder Dworack, the other ZL hadn't returned from the airport after sending off his old companion. With a little boost from the other two, I managed to open one of the windows and climb inside. Immediately, I started to think, "I sure hope this is the right house". As I stuck my head inside, I noticed a somewhat disturbing aroma inside. If you're familiar with the smell of a "porta-potty" or an outhouse; it was similar to that odor. Yuck!

Chapter 5: A Green-bean in Kagoshima

The three of us sat around in our new home, waiting for Dworack Choro to come back. As I mentioned back on the plane, "CHORO", CHO (long) RO (aged), is the literal translation for "Elder"; but sometimes this word would evoke odd looks from people, because it conjures the image of a leader or wise, elderly man. It wasn't too long before Dworack Choro was back. I'm sure he was a little surprised to find us inside the house. Dworack was a very interesting young man. He seemed a little more mature than other missionaries I had met thus far, and was a very good and loving missionary.

Dworack and I hit it off that very day. I soon discovered that he too enjoyed music and singing. Jeffery turned out to be a pretty good singer as well. Together, the three of us made up quite the little trio, if I do say so myself. Dworack had only one month to go, and was very excited to go home, just in time for Christmas. Nevertheless, he did manage to get one of his families baptized before his return.

The house that we lived in was a bit shabby and old. The flakey mold on the walls was a lovely light green. The wind made a melodic whistling sound as it found its way through the cracks over under, and through the sides of the house. Oh, and that smell? It was in fact the bathroom or more specifically, the toilet, or the lack thereof. We had what I later referred to as a "Plopper". It was simply a hole cut into the plywood floor, covered by a plastic lid. The hole was an opening into the open septic tank below. The odor that it emitted tended to make my trips to the bathroom very brief.

I was soon told the story of a certain green-bean that, while attempting to close the lid of our plopper, lost his white handbook, his alien registration, and a little cash; all of which fell out of his shirt pocket and into the pit. They say that although he had made a desperate attempt to retrieve his belongings, he was forced to watch them as they disappeared deeper into the abyss. I wondered if this story wasn't fabricated. But I was told that missionary was an Elder Peterson, who was at the time, serving in the same zone here in Kagoshima.

I met Elder Peterson at a couple of meetings, but I could never find the proper moment to verify whether the story was true or not. Years later, I had the opportunity to live and work in North Logan, UT. I became curious when I found that my kids had become acquainted with a boy at school with the same first and last name as that elder. I had one of my kids enquire about it, and the boy turned out to be the son of that same Elder Peterson. I have since been able to verify that "the plopper incident" was in fact true.

At the Kagoshima house, we walked or rode the bus if we ever wanted to go anywhere. Our house sat at the top of a very, very large hill. It was long decided that bikes were not practical in the area. The very bikes themselves were the other reason; they were rusty from top to bottom, flat tires, broken brake cables, and covered with ash from the nearby volcano, Sakura-jima; worst of all, they were only five-speeds. Although they were parked in plain sight, I never thought to ask anyone about those bikes. Frankly, I didn't want to know. *(More about the bikes later…)*

While I wasn't the best of students back at the MTC, I thought I had gained enough language ability that was at the very least, sufficient to get around with. I was sure that I had somewhat mastered the general salutations and other initial conversational tools. With little effort, I could greet anyone on the street or at the door with a KONNICHIWA (hello), or a KONBANWA (good evening). My delivery was pretty good, or so I thought. Nevertheless, I soon came to realize my lack of ability while on the receiving end of the conversation. "This is not what they taught me back at the MTC"[25], I must have said a million times in the first couple of days.

When people spoke to me, the words seemed garbled. I couldn't pull out one word from the other because it sounded like one continuous string of sounds. My head buzzed with confusion and frustration. I was learning vocabulary that wasn't even found in my trusty

[25] Reference to a line in "The Best Two Years", Halestorm Entertainment

little blue dictionary. Unfortunately it wasn't until some years later, through my studies at college, that I was able to ascertain the reason for some of the frustration that I was experiencing. I learned that the Kagoshima dialect or SATSUMA-BEN had a notable history. It is thought by some that during the Edo Period (1600's to the mid 1800's); this dialect was actually developed in order to identify spies coming from other areas of the country. This made perfect sense, after the fact. Had I known this at the time, I may not have been stressed so much about my inabilities. I couldn't have been expected to understand that babble.

In reality, what I was really going through was perfectly normal. With only eight weeks of language study, no one is expected to completely grasp Japanese, or any language for that matter. It would be up to me to put in the time, if I ever wanted to understand this language. I was eventually able to assimilate my language study to the area's dialect in a relatively short time. Throughout my mission, I found that there were many dialects yet to be learned on the island of Kyushu.

Aside from the dialect, I learned a few more things regarding my language study. I soon found that it was much easier to communicate with the children rather than their grown-up counterparts. The adults tended to think that it was their unsolicited duty to help me, by correcting my horrible Japanese <u>all the time</u>. This only seemed to add an extra element of embarrassment and frustration to certain situations.

To illustrate my point; one day at the park, there were a couple of young mothers sitting on a bench by their baby strollers. Upon greeting them, I exerted some courage and mentioned to one mother how cute her baby was. The word for "cute" in Japanese is "KAWAII". That was the word I meant to say, obviously. But the word that came out of my mouth was "KOWAI", which means "frightening". Clearly this was a huge gaffe on my part. Yet, instead of overlooking it and moving on, the young mother, full-well knowing what I had meant to say, felt the need to point out my mistake. I can only imagine the shades of red showing in my complexion. It seemed as though whenever I conversed with adults, the conversation would always turn into a little language lesson; by the time the lecture was over, I had already forgotten my original train of thought.

In contrast to the adults, the kids always excused the numerous flaws in my speech, only occasionally correcting me along the way. There was no major case made out of every little blunder. They simply enjoyed the conversation as it was. I grew to love the little ones more and more. Whenever we got the chance, Jeffery Choro and I would make our way to the park to play with the kids. They were, without a doubt, my very best teachers.

When we first arrived in Kagoshima, Jeffery and I didn't have a single investigator, no contacts, nothing. We were to open a new area for ourselves. I think this was a particularly exciting challenge for Jeffery Choro. I also think that he and I did the hardest tracting that I would ever do throughout the rest of my mission.

In addition to the alarm clock, the letter from the Missionary Department included a list of essential clothing to bring as well. It did include a mention of winter clothing. But for some reason, what I had brought was lacking… in spite of the fact that Kagoshima was at the southernmost point of the island of Kyushu; its latitude is only about one degree north of sunny San Diego, California.

Nevertheless Kagoshima seemed painfully cold to me. Being from the Pacific Northwest, I thought I knew cold. Perhaps it was because I didn't go out for long walks in it. With no central heating, it was just as cold inside the house as it was outside. So I ended up using all of my money in the first couple of days, just buying an overcoat and gloves. Nevertheless, with a small loan from my loving companion, I was able to make do until my funds had arrived.

At this point, I think I will tell you a bit more about Jeffery Choro. I was so blessed to have him as my trainer. Had it not been for him, my mission might have been a complete disaster, or at least much more difficult. In our first ten hours of tracting, we knocked on two-hundred and thirty doors. I know this because I counted each and every one. I listened to my companion give his door approach over and over until I knew every line verbatim; yet not one time did he make me take on a single door.

On about the third day I finally asked him why he didn't want me to do an approach. He replied, "I'm just waiting for you to want to do it on your own". He probably figured that if he forced me do it, I might have resented him for pressuring me. Actually, he might have been right. So, with a nod from my loving companion, I knocked on the very next door by myself. I probably should have waited a little longer because, from that time forward, I was obligated to do nearly every other door. Suddenly the work became very hard and real for me.

We did what was called the "Blessing Approach". The Blessing Approach was when you ask the person at the door if we might offer a blessing on the household right there in the GENKAN or entry way. Actually, for most Japanese homes, it is not uncommon to have a Shinto Priest or KANNUSHI come into one's house to offer a purification ritual or blessing known as HARAI. But for LDS missionaries, it was a relatively new thing. Of course, this approach was designed to evoke questions and hopefully lead to a comeback.

Of the two-hundred and thirty apartments, we managed to do seven blessings. From those, we only had a single return visit. Eventually, we found one family that would actually allow us to begin teaching them. It was the Fukuishi family. They had two little boys; one was about four and the other maybe six.

I remember trying to teach part of a lesson to them, and how scared I was. Our meetings with them went well, even to the point of getting them to come to church. There was only one snag with that. When they arrived on Sunday, for some reason their youngest son thought that the church was a hospital. He screamed and screamed, refusing to go inside. Embarrassed, the family ended up going home. They never did come back, at least while I was there.

In our quest to build a teaching pool, we made contact with a variety of interesting people. At one of the doors we entered, a woman invited us in after our blessing. She had a couple of kids inside, but apparently no husband. After sitting down, we tried hard to carry on a conversation, soon realizing that she was not what one might consider "stable". Even the kids seemed a little uncomfortable at the situation.

We decided it would be best to leave, but when we tried to excuse ourselves, the woman began offering us various objects. I think she felt she owed us for the blessing. First, she handed Jeffery a bird in a small cage, but he managed to talk her out of that. Finally, she forced me to take a thousand yen bill by stuffing it into my hand. We were already making our way towards the door at this point and began bowing; we hurried to get our shoes on. As she bowed, I was able to hand the money to one of the kids standing behind her. What a relief it was to get away from there.

In time we were able to accumulate a small number of people that we could visit on a regular basis. Yet not all were interested in hearing the gospel. One particular man that we often visited was quite obviously intoxicated each time we came. Nevertheless, he really seemed to enjoy our company.

After being in Kagoshima nearly two weeks, I was hit with an epiphany. Is it possible that you might have already figured it out by now? If you recall, before I entered the MTC, I had met a young Japanese exchange student named Yasuyuki. Going through my things, I found the address that he had written down for me. I realized that I had in fact made it to the very same city that he lived in. I showed the address to Elder Dworack, who located it on the map for us. The following afternoon, Jeffery and I took the bus to that general area and began our search.

After walking for quite a while, we finally reached what Jeffery Choro believed to be Yasuyuki's neighborhood. Without actually seeing the Chinese characters (Kanji) Jeffery tried to imagine how the name Chuman, which was the boy's last name, would read in Japanese. According to Jeffrey, this name was not a typical Japanese name. We stopped at each house. At most of the homes, one could go right up to the door. But there was one particular house that seemed unique from the others.

The house had a front gate leading into a little driveway. Inside the gate was a barking Doberman. I didn't realize it at the time, but that type of gated home, especially with a Doberman Pinscher is a very rare site. Jeffery Choro thought that it might be the place, but there was no way to know for sure. There were no signs indicating "Chuman" and the dog was getting increasingly agitated. Just as we were deciding whether to leave or not, a small truck came up to the gate. We stopped them to ask if the boy Yasuyuki lived there. Before the man could answer, I saw a boy sticking his head out of one of the windows of the house. He began waving and calling my name. It was Yasuyuki. I couldn't believe this was actually happening.

It would have made perfect sense had I awakened that very moment. It was so wonderful to be able to see him again. But at least I could communicate a little better with him this time. Without hesitation, his parents invited us inside for a little while. We had a very enjoyable visit with this amazing little family. Consequently, they fell in love with us and invited us back for dinner the following Sunday. Who would have thought or even imagined that the Lord would see fit to make this reunion possible. What other explanation is there? What are the odds of this being an accident?

My first experience at church on Sunday was somewhat interesting. There were six elders in our district. The other two elders from across town attended our Branch as well. The senior companion was Romney Choro, the junior was Poole Choro. If Romney Choro's last name seems familiar it's because he is a grandson of President Marion G. Romney, the first counselor to the prophet, Spencer W. Kimball. He was a tall, handsome young man and would later become one of my dear friends in the mission. Poole Choro, who would also become a friend, was from Las Vegas.

Poole was a little like me, just a little cynical and defiant. There was one time he had let his hair grow maybe a little too long for missionary standards. Apparently the Buch or his wife made a comment to him about this at a zone conference. I suppose Poole Choro chose not to take the criticism very well. At the next conference he was seen with a shaved head. He surely had some guts.

On one particular Sunday we were all sitting in the back row of the small chapel during the Sacrament Meeting. A certain young sister was being recognized for something at the pulpit with the branch president. I think she was moving up from the Young Women's organization. All of a sudden a number of the members began to clap their hands right there in the chapel. A couple of the missionaries tried in vain to get them to stop. It was so interesting to see some of the differences in the Church across the globe. Of course the truths were all the same; but sometimes you could see that some of the most taken-for-granted things had lost a little in translation. Of course these days, those differences have pretty much gone away.

On another occasion, we were having a discussion about keeping the Sabbath Day holy in the Priesthood meeting. Dworack Choro's investigator, Brother Matsumoto was sitting with us. He and his wife were to be baptized the following Sunday. When the question was posed, "What kinds of activities are appropriate to do on Sunday?"; several of the brothers began their replies, including such things as scripture study, home teaching, and attending Church meetings. Brother Matsumoto raised his hand and explained that he works six days a week; Sunday was his only day off.

Brother Matsumoto continued to say that he and his boys really enjoyed going to the park to play catch. The other brothers all but jumped on top of him. From what I could gather, they seemed to be informing him that those days would be over once he had become a member. We all could see the confused look on Brother Matsumoto's face and could imagine what he must have been feeling. About then, Romney Choro raised his hand saying that he knew that one of the priorities of keeping the Sabbath Day holy was spending time together as a family.

Romney continued by sharing that some of his fondest memories as a small child were the times when his Grandpa (President Romney) would come over and shoot hoops with the boys before dinner on Sunday. There was a pregnant pause, and then the topic of the lesson somehow switched to the importance of family unity. Brother Matsumoto and his beautiful family were nevertheless baptized that very next week. I might add that it sure felt great to see my first baptisms performed in Japan.

I came to Japan just sixteen days before Thanksgiving. Any return missionary can describe their first string of holidays away from home, regardless of where they went. Our Thanksgiving dinner was held four days early at our zone conference. Stoneman was there; that alone made it a little homier for me. The food tasted pretty good but that evening, I was feeling a little sick. Perhaps I ate too much. That was probably the first night that we didn't go out tracting.

The odd thing was that nothing particularly special happened on Thanksgiving; it was just another day in Japan. That is likely when I started to feel the subtle twinges of homesickness. For some reason, I imagined that I would get a call from home. No such luck; now it was on to Christmas, the one day that had always been the highlight of my year. For the next few weeks, any type of mail made my heart race. Yet, the days that brought no mail seemed to bring me down a little.

Dworack Choro's mom, who was planning to get re-married soon, called quite often in the middle of the night. Calls in the night usually meant calls from America. I always found it hard to get back to sleep on those nights. Dworack was going home in time for Christmas. Boy was I jealous. I suppose my letters to home might have caused some concern to my parents. In my dad's usual subtle way, I was comforted to have him to remind me why I was sent there.

> Dear Peter,
>
> Your letter this week had a ring to it, like the old Pete that we knew. It's good to hear that you are able to communicate with your favorite people now. I too much prefer little children to grownups. It's an amazing coincidence that you happen to have wound up in the same city as that exchange student. Perhaps it's not just a coincidence, but rather something more profound.
> It's really strange how mortal we really are. You and I both know that you're where you should be, doing what you should do. But even so, I miss you and can't help wishing you were home. I hope that all your life, no matter where you are, you'll still want to come home. I hope it will always be a place where you know you can come and be welcome to just be yourself… We feel really good about you and your attitude and I want you to know, I couldn't be more proud of you for the way you have met this challenge… At least I can proudly say that all my sons have been men enough

to go out and preach our religion to the world. God bless you son and BE HAPPY.

Love Dad

On his last P-day, Dworack invited me to go with him and a member down to the southernmost part of Kyushu, Ibusuki. We went to the ocean and then we ate. Although I had never eaten sparrow eggs or eel before, it was surprisingly good. I truly enjoyed the last bit of time I could spend with Dworack before he went home. When he did go in December, it left a vacancy for a zone leader in the house. To my surprise, it would be Jeffery Choro who would be filling that vacancy. This of course meant that I would get a new SEMPAI or senior. On top of that, I would also be getting my first Japanese companion.

I had only been out a month, and not sure if I was ready for this. My new companion was Tomita Choro. He was a skinny, quiet, twenty-seven year old man, with a master's degree… in Physics. I don't think that the Buch could have found a better contrast of a companion for me. In a matter of a couple of hours, I realized that I may have found my complete opposite doppelganger, if there is such a thing. His hobbies were Japanese Chess, reading books, and guess what? He enjoyed bicycling too.

Besides our common belief in the Gospel, it was pretty hard for me to find much in common with Tomita Choro. My first night together with him was an interesting one. He seemed likable enough; yet we didn't communicate very well. It was definitely best when the four of us were together. When it was just the two of us, in order to be understood, we ended up playing a lot of charades and doodling on paper.

For some reason Tomita had gotten it in his head that it was his duty to "SYL" or Speak Your Language like we had to do back at the MTC. I guess he figured that it would be better for me if he spoke only Japanese, yet I was quite sure that he could speak at least a little English. I suppose that I felt that he was just being cruel to me. After dinner that first night, we just stayed in. Jeffery moved his stuff out of our room as Tomita got himself settled in. Then it was bed time.

You may not believe what happened next. The lights were turned off. I said my prayers, and then rolled over in my Futon[26]. I said "OYASUMI NASAI TOMITA CHORO", "Good night Elder Tomita", and he returned the same words back to me. In less than a minute the strangest thing happened. Tomita Choro began inhaling with deep breaths one after the other; each time he would hold his breath a little longer than before; he continued this until it appeared that he had passed out. He had knocked himself out! I wanted to get out

[26] Unlike the type of futon sold in typical U.S. furniture stores, a futon is more like a thick, quilt-like pad with a lighter quilt on top.

of there, I'm not kidding.

It turned out that this would be Tomita's nightly ritual. Perhaps he learned that sleep method in grad school. In addition to this, mornings for Tomita came very early, THREE O'CLOCK IN THE MORNING EARLY! That was when the light directly above my head came on. I suppose I wasn't very pleased with this situation. Nevertheless, our communication situation being what it was, I decided I would have to bear with it for the time being.

For the entire previous month, it was understood that we didn't use the bicycles. Yet the first morning after his arrival, I saw my new companion outside, dusting off those rusty old five speeds. "What the heck is he doing?" I thought. After just one day, it became obvious to me that Tomita was almost obsessively clean and tidy, yet what possible reason would he have to clean the bikes? Like I said, it was understood that the purpose of those bikes were to merely sit and gather the ash that spewed from our local volcano, Sakurajima.

The tires on these old bikes were flat; I'm sure the brakes were shot. And we all knew that this area was not designed to be traversed by bicycle. Nevertheless, there he was, working on those five-speeds. Apparently he had managed to find a tire repair kit, a pump, and various tools that were lying around the house. In just a couple of hours he had converted a pile of junk into two functioning bicycles.

In retrospect, I suppose I was completely oblivious to just how industrious Tomita Choro was. "Morris Choro, IKIMASHO" (Let's go), he called from atop his bicycle seat. Unfortunately for me, I didn't know how to articulate what I really wanted to say. So like a mindless drone, I got on that bike and rode off with him. He cheerfully rode along, with a map in one hand, carefully calculating the best route to take. Down the hill we went, almost flying.

We went through and across what seemed like the entire city of Kagoshima. The ride was interesting and almost enjoyable; that is until we decided to head for home. Pointing at the map, I believe that Tomita Choro was trying to show me what he thought to be the best way home. Supposedly, it would be the route with the most gradual incline. It didn't really matter because any way we went would be an unbearable climb, at least for me. Even if I did know how to say it, I doubt that there was any way I could have convinced Tomita to ditch the bikes and catch a taxi back or something.

As we approached the hill, I had already decided that it was going to be an impossible task for me. We stopped at the bottom and looked up at the winding road. After a minute or two, Tomita began pedaling upwards with no apparent effort. Somewhat impressed, I got on my bike, and began pedaling too. My pedals made it around about fifteen or twenty revolutions, and then gradually slowed to a complete halt. My bike eventually wilted over to one side and I ended up pushing it the rest of the way. I could see Tomita watching me from above for what seemed to be about twenty-five minutes.

For the next few mornings, there he would be, sitting on his bike, waiting for me to join him. I tried several times to tell him, in English, that I didn't think it was fair that we had to ride so much. He just wouldn't listen. He would just say things back to me in Japanese. I suppose I wasn't listening either. If I wanted things to change, it would require a little more effort on my part. So I woke myself up early one morning and prepared a little speech, completely in Japanese. In it, I simply stated my views on the practicality, or rather the impracticality of riding bikes in this area.

With Tomita already perched on his bike, I carefully read my short proclamation. He listened intently, even helping me with minor corrections to my wording. He nodded his head; then very slowly and carefully told me that he didn't mind just riding bikes once in a while. He then dismounted his bike and motioned for me to walk with him.

All that wasted time busting my buns on that rust bucket of a bike and hating it; if only I had acted sooner, I could have saved myself a lot of grief and strained muscles. I felt a great sense of accomplishment at that moment. So from that day forward, I decided to use the language I was sent there to use. The more effort I put into doing that, the easier things became. With that issue resolved, our companion relationship actually developed quite nicely. This was in spite of his nightly ritual, which for some reason I managed to get used to.

Each day, as we walked along together, my speaking and reading ability increased dramatically. Tomita would point out objects all day long, teaching me the vocabulary. As we passed houses, he taught me how to read the characters of the names written on the nameplate at the entryway. I am sure that in one month, he taught me what normally might have taken three or four months to learn.

In mid-December, we went to my first multi-zone conference. It was quite a long train ride to Kumamoto. Nearly all the missionaries from our zone rode together. I made one of my best friends in the mission on the train that day. Sister Kunugi was her name. We seemed to hit it off right from the start and ended up talking the entire way. Our conversation actually started with her correcting my lousy Japanese. With the exception of my companion, most of the Japanese missionaries had been too polite to say anything. Instead of letting me slide by with nearly the right words, Kunugi would step up and make me say it correctly. But she didn't do it in an embarrassing way like the ladies at the park. She could do it in such a way that we both were laughing about it.

Sister Kunugi helped me through some of

my toughest times. For the rest of my mission, she would be one of my crutches whenever I needed encouragement.

The conference was a wonderful break from the daily routine and I was able to reunite with some of my MTC friends. Stoneman, Wright, Thomas, and Dallimore were all there. We did skits, watched some videos, and ate really good food for a change. Without a doubt, the highlight of the conference was when the Buch dressed up like Santa Clause. Each missionary got to sit on his lap and receive a package that he and Sister Shimizu had arranged to have sent from home.

The Buch had previously written a letter to all the families of the missionaries, asking them to send a package to be opened at the conference. I got a package from both Mom and Grandma. I could feel my mom's love as I looked through each little item in the box. I was so full of nostalgia that I must have appeared somewhat giddy. It was so good to be with Stoneman again too. That night, we laid on our futons and talked for over an hour.

The next morning we got up for a testimony meeting. I ended up being the last to stand up. I felt a strong spirit as I reflected on the blessings of Jesus Christ, especially at that time of year. I felt that I was part of a pretty good bunch of missionaries. I had made some real friends there in Kagoshima.

Christmas happened to fall on a Sunday that year. We Americans opened the still wrapped presents left over from our packages. We all decided to save them until Christmas morning. After church, Yasuyuki's family came and took us to a charity party. Apparently, we were pictured in a newspaper article about.

There are only two times that missionaries are allowed to call home, Christmas and Mother's day. We were nearly a day ahead of those in the States, so Monday for us was Christmas back home. The missionary apartments had pink pay phones in them. This way we could pay the bill with the money that we had already deposited for our calls. With these particular phones, in order to call overseas and reverse the charges, it was necessary to turn a key in the back, making it a regular phone. Unfortunately, the key for our phone happened to be missing. Since we could not call overseas, it was necessary for us to contact our folks and have them call us instead.

A few doors down from our house lived a member of our branch. I had never seen her at church, but we could sometimes see her coming home from work early in the morning. She was always friendly to us. Not that I was paying attention to such things, but she was also fairly young and pretty. Anyway, back to the phone problem.

The night before it was to be Christmas back home, we decided we should go to the neighboring sister's house and make quick collect calls to our families. We would then instruct them to call <u>us</u>, rather than our calling them collect. When it was my turn to call, it was my mom that answered the phone. We had previously agreed by mail that I would make the call to my grandma's house later that day. This way, everyone would be available to talk with me. So when I attempted to make my call, Mom actually refused to accept the charges, thinking that I had made a chronological error. Instead, she asked the operator to relay a message, telling me to call Grandma's house later in the day. In return, I asked the operator to relay a message instructing them to call me instead.

As I heard the operator relay the message to my mom, it seemed that everything went okay. Yet very early the next morning, we were awakened by that sister down the street. Through the door, she was shouting about an overseas call for me at her house. Half asleep, I jumped up, threw on my overcoat, and then ran outside. What was I thinking? There I was following this pretty young sister along the wet winter street and into her home. If I recall, in my haste, I wasn't even wearing shoes.

As I entered her house I could see that the phone was on the floor… next to her futon. When I picked up the receiver, I suddenly realized what was going on. My dad was on the other end saying, "Hello Pete, sit back and get ready to talk to everybody!" That previous night, the operator must have given my mom the number of that sister's phone instead of ours. Now wide awake, I quickly assessed the situation.

I was alone, kneeling on the floor next to the young woman who was now crawling back into her bed. Without hesitation, I responded by giving him the correct number and saying, "Hang up and call me back in five minutes". To the best of my ability, I thanked the kind sister and apologized for the terrible inconvenience. If anyone had been outside watching, I shudder to think what they might have thought. I suppose it looked like I was sneakily tip-toeing back to our house, but in reality my feet were just freezing on the wet December pavement. The family eventually called me back as instructed. I was able to talk to everyone there.

Aside from all the confusion, that phone call was most definitely the best part of my Christmas that year. As missionaries, we tried our best to make Christmas special for the members. American missionaries were always asked to share stories of the Christmases they enjoyed as kids. Our Christmas spirit always seemed to rub off on everyone. Nearly every American elder I knew was asked to dress like Santa at one time or another. A Christmas carol in English was always a treat as well.

Our knowledge of the season was most valuable to those members. To the largely non-Christian Japan, Christmas is focused on Santa Clause and the general commercial aspects of the season. An average Japanese family might pause to eat cake or open simple presents. But without a thought of the real meaning of

Christmas, it was just another day. I have never appreciated Christmas as much as when I was in Japan.

Dear Pete,

This is the last letter I'll be writing to you this year. As I write this letter you are about to wake up to New Year's Eve. I hope you aren't planning any wild party… It was sure good to hear your voice last Sunday and know that everything is okay with you. I would like you to do me a favor though. I'd like for you to go to the neighbor we called and apologize for my waking her up. I'm sure it must have been a real shock for her to hear nothing but English on the other end.
I'm sitting here eating yogurt. I'll bet you never thought you'd see the day when your old dad would eat that pansy stuff. I've recently become the father of a bouncing baby ulcer, so I have to eat it. I did have a chilidog last night but it nearly did me in… Well I've got to go but you just "keep on keeping on" and the time will fly. We love you. Bye for now.

Love Dad

Without question, the most celebrated

holiday in Japan would have to be New Years. It is the time of the year when families get together to share in the celebration of a new beginning. The moms spend hours and energy making O'SECHI RYORI or New Year's foodstuff. I imagine that missionaries are fed the most during that wonderful week of celebration. That New Years for me meant the beginning of a complete year in Japan. At last I was starting to get that total feeling of newness out of me. Rollings Choro would be on his way home in a few days. In celebration, I baked the precious cherry chip cake mix that I got in my Christmas box to commemorate his successful mission. I put candles on it to represent each month he served.

During that New Year's week, we were told not to do regular proselytizing. People were busy, and most had guests in their homes. It was nice to have a little break anyway. But believe it or not, we did manage to keep busy. Members were very kind to invite us into their homes. We also spent some time with Yasuyuki's family and were even able to teach them a little. We developed a special friendship with that beautiful family. Yasuyuki's dad was especially warm to me, making me feel like one of the family.

Later in the week, we organized a bowling party with our English class, which included a few members. That day was also the day before Rowlings was to go home. I would really miss him. Surprisingly, I received something that I least expected on that day as well. It was my first transfer call from the Buch. That was the last thing I wanted to do just then; I was just getting used to being there. Everyone else was shocked as well.

I had only been in Kagoshima two measly months. I had just begun to settle in, getting used to my companion, and just starting to figure out the language. To my surprise, within a few minutes after I hung up with the Buch, I got a call from Romney Choro. It turned out that he was leaving as well. He and I would be riding the long 7 hour trip to Fukuoka together. I was being transferred to a place called Futsukaichi, and I only had one day to get my stuff together and say all my goodbyes. I called everyone I could think of.

Later that same day, we went downtown to say goodbye to Yasuyuki's family at their restaurant. Mr. Chuman told me to take care of myself, and that I could call him if I ever needed anything. I saw a little tear in his eye; I think he felt a sort of fatherly feeling toward me. That was very comforting to me. I left some small gifts with the two kids, hugged Yasuyuki, and went on my way.

Chapter 6: Not So Green in Futsukaichi

Morning came quickly and we made our way down to the train station. All the missionaries in our district and a bunch of members came to see us off. In his usual detail-minded manner, Tomita Choro had prepared a map of the station where I was to get off, complete with meticulous walking directions to the apartment in Futsukaichi. Although it was a hand written map, it looked like something you might buy at a bookstore.

Leaving Kagoshima was very, very hard. It had been my first home in Japan; yet knowing that Romney Choro and I would be traveling together made leaving a little easier; traveling together was quite enjoyable. In fact we were laughing most of the way. As soon as we were settled in our seats, Romney asked if I wanted to listen to some music on his Walkman. He then pulled out a cassette tape labeled "John Denver". While it may not have been one of my top choices, I figured it was better than nothing at all. He inserted the tape and handed me one of his ear buds. I may be mistaken, but as I recall, that music sounded a little more like Led Zeppelin than John Denver. Whenever we had the chance to meet up, Elder Romney never failed to surprise me on other occasions as well.

At one point along the way, I would need to transfer trains in order to get to Futsukaichi; and thanks to Tomita's map, I made it to the new apartment without a hitch. I was surprised how different the atmosphere was there. Unlike Kagoshima, we lived very close to the train station as well as many stores and restaurants. It seemed so much busier. My new companion had only been out two months ahead of me. His name was Marshall Choro, yet another companion from Utah. We transferred in at the same time, so neither of us knew the area at all. The Elders we were to replace would stay with us for a few days until we had met with all the investigators. One of the elders would be transferring stateside. It turned out that he and Japan were not very compatible. Things in Japan can sometimes feel a little closed-in and tightly spaced. Apparently these particular attributes didn't exactly agree with this elder. He would be going to Spokane, Washington. It really doesn't get much more wide open than that.

Futsukaichi is more or less a suburb of the city of Fukuoka, the biggest city on the island. Within walking distance were a McDonalds, a Mister Donut, and a large department store called UNEED. You could see Uneed from our front door, situated on the other side of a large canal. The water in the canal was only a few inches deep, but the cement structure itself was about 8 feet in depth and probably 15 feet in width. In front of the store's parking garage stood an elderly man in a uniform. I guess he was some sort of security guard or parking attendant. Whenever we looked over, there he was… day or night.

Our apartment was on the second story of a somewhat older apartment building. It had two bedrooms, with a bath and a toilet. We didn't have a shower like we had in Kagoshima. Instead we had a bath tub. Bath tubs in Japan are usually a bit different than those we have in the States. The one that we had was almost cubed shape, making the depth fairly deep. It also had a lid on it to keep the water hot and clean. In a typical Japanese household, bathers used a large bowl to dip into the tub. They would then pour the hot water over their head while standing up or sitting on a stool on the tile floor, in which there is a drain. Then the person would lather up, and then rinse off in the same manner. Only when they were clean, would one get into the tub to soak. In the missionary apartments however, the bather would do everything in that same manner, minus the soaking part. Standing on that tile floor, with no central heating in the house; the temptation to submerge one's freezing naked body in early January was very hard to resist sometimes.

The idea behind our not soaking in the tub was to save the bath water for the next day, and hopefully keep it as clean as possible for the next person. You may recall the type of toilet we had in Kagoshima, "the Plopper"? Well the toilet in Futuskaichi was one step up from that. We called this type of toilet a "squatter". On a completely tiled floor, one had to step up to where the toilet was. It had the appearance of a narrow turned over porcelain urinal. By its name, I don't think I need to explain its usage.

For nearly a week, we shadowed the incumbent elder until his transfer was carried out. We spent the better part of that week teaching at various English classes that the previous string of missionaries had accumulated. Some of them were at the church and some were at peoples' homes. It seemed like we spent an awful lot of time just doing that. The apartment was meant to be a four-man, but for the time being, after our predecessors were gone, it was just the two of us. While I now realize that it was sort of against regulation, for a month or so we both had our own rooms.

Fortunately we started out with more investigators here than we did in Kagoshima. Of course we didn't have any in Kagoshima. Many investigators here had been visited and taught by the missionaries for a long time. On the fourth day, we visited an elderly widow, Fujiki-san. She turned out to be a very unique lady. Each week on the same day, the elders had a standing appointment at her house for lunch. I believe she felt it was her duty to expose us to the more interesting cuisine of Japan upon each visit. The entrée on our first visit included miso soup. Today, many people in the States know this soup. But I don't know of many who would eat it if it had little fish heads in it. On another occasion, she presented us with a variety of sushi.

You may know what NIGIRI ZUSHI is. It is

basically a molded clump of seasoned rice with a piece of something on top. Much of it was pretty good, yet some, for a lack of a better term, sort of repulsed me. The easy ones to eat were the boiled shrimp and raw tuna (most popular among missionaries). I also liked the SABA or seasoned mackerel (cooked). The ones that I just couldn't bring myself to eat were the roe or fish egg ones.

There were two types of roe that I often came across: the salmon eggs; when I looked at them, I could only see the bait we used for trout fishing when I was growing up; they were red or orange and came in a small jar. How could I possibly put that into my mouth? Next, we have UNI (pronounced OONEE). Uni are tiny eggs which are harvested from the inside of a sea urchin. Later I realized that uni was somewhat of a delicacy, as sushi goes. Even so, to this day, I have only had it once and I doubt I ever will again.

As we ate the sushi, Fujiki-san continued to enter and exit the room, bringing in more delicacies. When the uni was placed before me, I searched my dictionary to see what it was. I then told Marshall Choro that I couldn't bring myself to eat it. So as Fujiki-san left the room I took a handkerchief, wrapped it around the uni, and casually slipped it into my suit pocket.

Now we still had a number of other places to go before we would get back to the apartment; it was a matter of hours before we got home. Of course I had forgotten about the uni in my pocket. In the end, my suit would need good long soaking in the sink and lots of soap before I could wear it in public again.

We really did come to love sweet little Fujiki-san. While she truly loved the teachings of the Gospel, she told us that she could never join the Church. She used a myriad of excuses: She was too old, her friends would disavow her, or even that her dead husband might not approve of it. Nevertheless, I will never forget her sweet spirit. It was like going to my grandma's house every week.

Now that it was just the two of us, Marshall Choro and I plugged along for the next couple of weeks. We were making moderate progress with some of our investigators, but no major developments were ever seen. Thanks to Tomita Choro, I could safely say that my Japanese was at least as good as my senior companion's. But we ended up learning and sharing a lot together.

Mama,

I moved… But I wasn't happy to leave at all!! I guess I had a lot of reasons why. I have a companion from Utah. We get along great, but he's only been out here for four months and my Japanese is as good as or better than his (not bragging)… There are no trees here, it's all city. I'm shriveling up!
Sometimes I actually forget about it,

but Mom, I'm in Japan… Do you realize it? Japan!
We live right by the biggest shrine on Kyushu Island called "Da Zaifu" and tomorrow there is a big celebration for people turning 20 (seijinshiki). It'll go on till Monday too. We'll go down and take some pictures.
We have appointments nearly every night. Personally I'd rather be on my knees under a short table drinking hot milk and eating rice cake or little fish heads than going door to door asking people if we can bless their house… I think…
It's a lot more convenient for riding bikes here, but man does my butt hurt!! The seats are too small.
Anyway, you guys are all items of mention in my prayers. I hope you all are doing fine. Don't stop writing, ok? I start to drag until the letters come, then I'm alive for another week.
I love you all, you're great Mom, take care.

Love Pete (your little baby who longs to be in your arms)

On one particular P-day Marshall and I were doing our shopping across the canal at Uneed. We found ourselves separated for a few moments, when a young woman came up to me and began asking me questions. I must admit that I couldn't follow everything that she was going on about. She asked me if I was a BOKUSHI (preacher). I told her that a bokushi was close enough. She then said that she had a problem and wanted me to help her. Just then Marshall came along. "What's up?" he asked. I tried to repeat what she had said to me, but I'm sure the details were a little mottled.

Neither of us could understand exactly what this girl wanted, but it was clear that she was upset. Marshall suggested that we all go down to the church and have a little discussion. We dropped off our groceries at the apartment and walked down to the church building. Actually the building was a house being used as a church. As we got further into the conversation it became apparent what her problem exactly was.

The girl's name was Harumi. We learned that she was fifteen and living on her own. She had a job at a nearby hair salon as a hair washer. I had noticed that her hands seemed very raw and dry. I guess that was the result of the shampoo on her hands all day. She had moved away from home in the northern part of Kyushu some months before. The problem turned out to be her concern for her mother's wellbeing.

Harumi's mother was an alcoholic and in very poor health. The mother had evidently refused to get any help or treatment. Harumi was worried that her mother had reached a dangerous point and hoped that we could help her. Marshall told her that we weren't able to do anything in that way. I really couldn't argue the point, but it still didn't sit well with me. While I couldn't think of anything to do at the time, I told her that I would come up with something. Before parting, we exchanged phone numbers and then said our goodbyes.

We had another appointment that evening and all the while, I couldn't get my mind off of that poor kid's problem. Marshall and I struggled to come up with something that we could do. That night, I was impressed to call Sister Noma, who was in our branch. She happened to be the Stake President's wife. I explained Harumi's problem as best I could. Without hesitation, Sister Noma took down Harumi's phone number, saying that she would try to see what she could find out.

A couple of days went by and I got a phone call from our new young friend Harumi. She simply said, "Everything is going to be all right." And then she thanked me. I was somewhat confused and asked her what she was talking about. She went on to explain how Sister Noma had contacted her. They had a long talk about her mother's problem. Sister Noma became so concerned that she went quite the long distance to have a visit with Harumi's mother.

In short, with Sister Noma's promptings, the mother agreed to get herself admitted into a place where she could get some treatment for her problem. Harumi began to cry over the phone. She had never seen such kindness or concern by anyone like that before. I tried to explain that this is what people are supposed to do for one another. I also told her that this was the reason we were serving missions.

Right there over the phone, I had the opportunity to explain to Harumi about our Savior and his love for us. She was very receptive to the concept, and we commenced teaching her every Monday. Not only was it our P-day, but nearly all barber and beauty shops just happened to be closed on Mondays. Sometimes Sister Noma would even come and join the lessons. That was one time where I am sure that Heavenly Father had taken us by the hand and led us to one of his children who was in need. I am glad to have been there at that time and place.

When the usual day and time for transfer calls came, we were surprised to hear the phone ring. We had only been together about a month and it seemed strange that we might get a call. When my companion answered the phone, he said it was for me. My heart jumped, "No way! I just got here". That's what I was getting ready to say to the Buch; but when I got on the phone it was Stoneman. Now Stoneman had played tricks on the phone with me before.

As I mentioned earlier, we had pink pay phones in the apartments. As you are speaking, a buzzer would sound, telling you to insert another 10 yen coin. The further away the distance of the call was, the faster you needed to insert the coins. If you recall,

Stoneman was on a small, distant island. He had called me from there before; I could clearly hear him dropping the coins at a rapid rate. Just as he would drop the last coin, he would say something like, "You'll never guess what happened!" or "Oh yeah, I forgot to tell you…" and then the call would be cut off. This of course would force me to have to call him right back to get the news. When the phone connected, he would be laughing and then say something like, "Oh I just wanted to see if you'd call back…"

When I heard Stoneman's voice on the phone, I suspected that he might have something up his sleeve. But it turned out that he was calling to tell me that he was becoming a senior, or rather a trainer for a "green bean". In our mission, it was very rare for a missionary who had only been in the field for four months. But Stoneman was pretty rare himself. I was so excited and happy for him. He further went on to tell me that he was also transferring. He would be leaving for the Hombu to pick up his companion and then he would be going… to Futsukaichi. Stoneman was coming here! I was so excited. The following evening, Stoneman showed up with his greenie, Elder Walton. They would occupy the extra room, and Marshall would be back together with me.

The atmosphere took an amazing turn with these new Choros in our apartment. That first evening we just sat around and got familiar with one another. When Walton Choro discovered who I was he said, "I didn't think I'd be running into you so soon…" I struggled to recall whether or not I had ever known him before. It turned out that he was from South Carolina. In his final preparations before going into the MTC he had met my good friend Brad. Remember, he had gotten his call to South Carolina, the same day I got my call. Apparently Walton had been instructed by Brad, to locate me when he had the chance and say "Hi". What an odd coincidence… or not.

Stoneman would turn out to be a great trainer for Walton. I'm not entirely sure, but I believe Stoneman Choro was the first in our group to go senior. There may have been one other, but I think I am right. In order to become a senior in our mission you needed to pass a test of sorts with the APs. You were randomly given a lesson to pass off, in addition to a couple of scriptures. It was pretty hard to accomplish, yet I'm not surprised that Stoneman was able to do it so quickly.

Stoneman's going senior made me want to pass off even more. I began cramming the lessons into my brain as fast as possible. I carried them around and read them as we walked. I thought I was pretty close one time at a zone conference and tried to pass off, but I took a nose-dive. I knew I would have a chance again in about another week, so I continued to study. The APs had been scheduled to come to our apartment, so I made another appointment.

About two days before the APs were to come, I became very sick. I was so ill that I couldn't even stand up. I don't know what it was, but I was hit hard with it. We thought it might have been food poisoning or something. It got so bad that my pours began to emit a toxic odor. I even offended myself by it. When the APs came around, Marshall told them that I wasn't up to passing off. That was so disappointing, because I wasn't sure how long it would be before I would get another chance. Fortunately we were not far from the Hombu, which gave me more opportunities to try again.

The next few weeks flew by, now that Stoneman and I were together again. We did a lot of interesting things. Our first outing to the barber with the green-bean Walton was pretty memorable. Each of us got our hair trimmed and then it was Walton's turn. When the barber asked him how he wanted it cut, Walton looked to us for direction and support. Stoneman stepped in and told the barber to give him a "Supotsu Katto" or "Sports Cut". This is more or less a flat top or a buzz cut. Walton expressed a look of confusion, so Marshall and I assured him that the sports cut was what everybody gets. The barber pulled out his clippers and began mowing off Walton's hair before he even realized what was going on. Actually he didn't look all that bad with it. To my knowledge, that was Walton's look for the rest of his mission.

On another P-day, Stoneman woke up with the desire that we all go to a SENTO or public bath. These are not what are portrayed in the movies and such. Sentos are divided into men's and women's sections; it's perfectly legal for missionaries. Stoneman had wanted to go for quite some time and worked hard to convince us all to go. I had never been a big fan of sitting in nearly scalding hot water, but I agreed to go anyway.

We all got on our bikes and headed down the street. Marshall and I rode our brand new 18 speed bikes that the mission home had been distributing around the mission to replace the old bikes. Stoneman and Walton's bikes had not yet arrived so they were forced to ride our spare "Green Monsters". These were bikes that I'm sure, had been in the mission for at least fifteen or more years. They were "no-speeds"; they probably weighed 80 plus pounds, and seemed virtually indestructible. Rumor has it that a missionary once dropped a green monster off from a three story building, leaving not so much as a scratch on it.

As we rode down to the area of town where several sentos could be located, the owner or worker (mostly women) would call to us, inviting us in. We finally decided on one, as the woman there convinced us that her bath was top notch. As we entered the bath area in our birthday suits, eyes seemed to gravitate toward us. As I mentioned before, I was a fairly small person, but the other three were not small at all. You already know how big Stoneman was, but Marshall and Walton were not too much smaller in height, width, or girth.

The steamy room was already populated by a number of elderly men. Being the morning time, this was usually the main clientele for a sento; most people in Japan take their baths during the evening hours. Right away, a couple of us started to head straight for the big tub, only to be yelled at by the on looking men. They motioned for us to go and wash at the showers first. The showers were set low with a stool to sit on in front of a mirror. Each of us did as we were told and then went back towards the bath.

Stoneman was first to step into the nearly blistering water. As he sank deeper into the bath, the water level began to rise; Marshall entered next… the water was now brimming. When Walton got in, the water ebbed over the top spurring the laughter of our fellow bathers. Clearly it must have been a rare treat for them to see four white guys in the buff. When we all got out of the bath, we looked like boiled lobsters which brought on even more chuckles from our new found naked friends.

During our time together, Stoneman and I managed to find a number of opportunities to work together. We went on splits at least once a week. Not that I didn't want to be with my companion, but Stoneman was my best friend in the mission. In fact one day at Church Sister Koga, a woman in the branch, approached me about it. She asked why Stoneman and I seemed to enjoy being with each other more than our own companions. I explained that we were companions in the MTC. I guess it was obvious how close we had become. She asked if it would be weird to invite just the two of us to come to their house to visit. I guess it wasn't a problem because we went over that afternoon.

Sister Koga and her husband were very kind and interesting people. Theirs was the only house in Japan I had ever seen with a St. Bernard. Brother Koga came from a long family line that included actual Ninja. He practiced the ancient martial art of Kyusho Jitsu, which had been passed down for generations. He had a very old book for this art that had also been passed down to him. The main technique is the use of pressure points on a person's body. He showed that with one poke of a finger, you can knock out or kill a person. Ironically, as a profession Brother Koga happened to be a dress maker. Or perhaps that was just his cover...

The Kogas became very important to me even after my mission. The four of us were given special permission from the Buch to watch the Super Bowl at their house at two o'clock in the morning. The Kogas showed true love and compassion to me. Although, age wise, she could have been an older sister, Sister Koga was as good a substitute for a mom as anyone could have asked for.

Soon after Marshall and I reached Futsukaichi, we paid a visit to our district leaders' apartment to have a planning meeting. As soon as we entered, we noticed something out of the ordinary. There was a pile of food wrappers from McDonalds in their kitchen. Upon inquiry, we were shown the contents of their freezer; they had large supply of frozen hamburgers. They then explained to us that it was common knowledge around the mission that McDonalds threw away their unsold foodstuffs when they have either been sitting too long or when they close up for the evening. They don't simply dump the food directly into the trash though. They would neatly place the already wrapped items into a clean garbage bag, which is then closed up tightly. Those bags are placed into a larger garbage bag and deposited into the dumpster. We further learned that other fast food restaurants did the same sort of thing.

When Stoneman arrived at the apartment, we often spoke about the McDonalds' dumpster, but never acted upon it. Stoneman gradually became obsessed with the idea of raiding the dumpster of the neighboring Mr. Donut, thinking that they must also practice the same disposal practices. I suppose I too was somewhat enthusiastic, but not enough to get up in the middle of the night to do it. Nevertheless, one night before going to bed, Stoneman had concluded that we would go out. I told him that if he was willing to wake me, I'd go along. Consequently, Stoneman woke me a little after midnight.

To the best of my recollection, Stoneman was dressed in dark clothes like some kind if special ops commando. He rousted me up from a deep sleep, and out the door we went. As we approached the rear of the store, Stoneman identified the dumpster and then presented his plan. We would lurk our way to the dumpster where he would hoist me up. All I had to do was grab a bag or two. We were very careful not to be seen, because frankly I was a bit embarrassed about the whole thing.

Our plan was executed flawlessly, and we both scurried back into the dark at the edge of our apartment building. When I placed my hand into the bag to retrieve the goods, all that came back out was a handful of COFFEE GRINDS. I of course was disgusted and vowed to never do that again. Stoneman naturally got a big laugh out of that one.

Throughout my mission, I knew I could depend on Stoneman for moral support and true friendship. He depended on me once in a while too; like the time when he blew out the crotch in his pants while he and Walton were out working. He called me on the phone asking me to bring him another pair from his closet. The jokes from that day continued for some time.

On one particular morning during our study time, I was practicing new TANGO or vocabulary, (pronounced TAHNGO). I had previously put together lists of words according to topic. That day I was reviewing words that had to do with medicine and emergencies. Some of the tango included words like BYOUIN (Hospital), KUSURI (Medicine), KANGOFU (Nurse), and what turned out to be significant for me that day, KYUKYUSHA or ambulance.

Dear Mom,

> …last Wednesday or so we were coming home. As we crossed the railroad tracks by our house, I noticed a man lying on the ground. My companion was busy looking at a corvette that passed by. People were just walking by this man. I told my comp. to stop, so we parked our bikes and ran back. There was only one man trying to help this guy. He was hit by a car and had blood all over him. Well, finally some other guys stopped to help. They wanted to take him to the hospital in a taxi. So I had to run over to the train station and get in one, only to find out that the taxi driver wouldn't let him ride. He still made me pay 430 yen (about 2 bucks). Not sure, but I think I might have cussed at him in all the bad words I could think of (cont.)

The only other option was to try to find a phone and call for help. I ran over to a nearby bakery and asked the person there to call… that's right, a KYUKYUSHA (ambulance). What good timing to have learned the right word that very morning. I would be able to use that word at least one more time before the end of my mission (stay tuned for the rest of that story).

> (cont.…)Soon the ambulance made its

way through the traffic and picked him up. What a crazy night.
We're so darned busy! I can't believe it. We have five English classes, an appointment about every night, and a meal appointment at least once or twice a week. One lady likes to play Ping-Pong with us. That makes the time roll by. Sometimes too fast…
I guess this place is as good as anywhere to work, but I want baptisms!!
I hope everything is fine. I continually worry and pray about you all. Mom, I love you and thanks for remembering the oatmeal!! Tell Dad "hi" and that I love him. Take care.

Love Pete

It would turn out that Stoneman and I would only have a few more weeks together before I was to be transferred. I did manage to get passed off in the meantime. I could now go senior if only the Buch would let me. I enjoyed the time I spent with the other elders in our apartment as well. I had my twentieth birthday there with them. With the help of Stoneman (most likely), my birthday became common knowledge to everybody. As a result I was able to celebrate my birthday about four separate times that week. On the evening of my birthday, Stoneman had a cake decorated with my name and candles. He even blew up some plastic grocery bags as balloons.

Dear Pete (the birthday boy)

I'm glad you remembered Mom's birthday and the doll was really nice. I'm making a case for it so it won't get dirty. At least for one day on your mission you ate well. It sounds like you had quite a party. I hope some of those people are interested in the Gospel.
By the time you receive this you will be nearly out of your teens, your face will be clearing up now that you are no longer a teenager and people will undoubtedly start to call you "Sir". All in all it's a time of great excitement when our last child reaches 20 years of age. Makes you feel old doesn't it?
I hope you have a happy birthday and I wish I could be there with you.

Love Dad

On one P-day morning the phone rang. Marshall answered the phone and said it was for me; somebody named Pat. I thought, "My brother Pat?" When I answered the phone, it turned out to be another Pat. It was my friend Pat from back in high school and college. "Why on earth would you be calling me?" I asked. As it turned out, Pat had been on a cruise ship that just happened to be docked in Tokyo. He persistently located our phone number by calling my mom, and then the Hombu. What a surprising coincidence. The next time I would talk to Pat would be at our 25th High School reunion.

That following day we went to Fukuoka for a district meeting and a scheduled interview with the Buch. That might have been the reason for the transfer call two days later. I had been in Futsukaichi for a few months and had also passed off, so in some ways, I had anticipated the call. I suppose that I was a little surprised that I wasn't going senior. Instead, I would be getting another Japanese companion in a place called Hyuga. Hyuga is located in Miyazaki prefecture along the southeast coast. I was very sad to leave Futsukaichi. I had made a lot of friends there. Once again I would have to say goodbye not only to these new found friends, but also to Stoneman. The odds that Stoneman and I would find each other together again on the mission were not very good.

As it was in Kagoshima, I rushed around to say goodbye to everyone. We had two English classes that morning. This was the day after my birthday so at each place, there was a cake and great food. At one of the houses where we taught, some of the women sang and read poetry to me as a gift. I felt pretty special. Later we went to visit Harumi, the fifteen year old shampoo girl. We both wept, but she promised to keep studying the Gospel.

That evening we had a lesson appointment with one of our great investigators, Ishikura-san. Ishikura-san was a young married man with an adorable little baby boy. When he learned that I would be leaving the following day, he cut the lesson short. He wanted to play his favorite record album for me. Ishikura-san was a big Linda Ronstadt fan, and I always think of him when I hear her pretty voice. I had worked as a DJ at the college radio station back home and had mentioned how impressed I was with Ishikura-san's "old school" stereo system. He thanked me and then told us about one of his good friends who had an even better one. For some reason, he felt we should jump into his car and go over and take a look at it. So we did.

While I sat in the back seat, I thought how meeting Ishikura-san's friend might be a good missionary opportunity for us. When we arrived at the friend's door, we were graciously invited in. Stepping into the doorway, it appeared that Ishikura-san's friend had company, judging by the number of shoes there. As we entered the living room, we were able to match those shoes with their owners. "What are you doing here?" we heard, as Stoneman and Walton got up from the sofa. We echoed back the same question. This weird twist of fate was somewhat chilling. Who could have ever imagined that without each other's knowledge, we had been separately teaching two men? Two men, who lived completely across the city from each other, yet happened to be longtime friends. When we finally got over the surprise, we all sat and enjoyed a very good conversation on a wide spectrum of topics including, and most especially the Gospel.

That following morning, I packed up my stuff and got ready to leave. Marshall had me talk into a tape that he was compiling with the voices of all of his companions; I made him pose with my Washington state flag, as I did with all my companions.

Stoneman helped me get my stuff to the station on the back of his bike. A few investigators and friends were waiting for us there. One of our English students, Mrs. Inoue (the Ping-Pong player) brought food for me to take along for the ride. Stoneman and I hugged. Who knew if we would ever see each other again for the rest of our missions?

Chapter 7: Still a Junior in Hyuga

The train ride to Hyuga seemed extraordinarily long. It's probably because this was my first time traveling alone. I hadn't noticed just how much people seemed to stare at me until now. When I arrived at Hyuga, my new companion, Tomioka Choro was there to greet me. We quickly stashed my stuff at the house, and then went straight to the city office to adjust my status as an alien. That evening we had an appointment; I was assigned to teach the lesson with very little preparation. We stayed out pretty late; I was finally able to unpack at about 10:30. Tomioka Choro was a twenty-two year old from Tokyo. It didn't take long to adjust to him, but his Japanese seemed a little different somehow, especially in comparison to Tomita Choro.

Hyuga was a beautiful city on the ocean. Being near the ocean was a great change for me because I missed the salty air from back home. The missionary house was also used as the Church building. Our rooms were upstairs and we shared the kitchen and bathroom with the branch. The day after I arrived, I realized that I would be the sole teacher of our little English class, as it was only the two of us in this area.

My first Sunday in Hyuga was somewhat enlightening as well. It turned out that my companion and I made up the entire the Melchizedek Priesthood in addition to being the Branch Presidency. Tomioka Choro was the Branch President, which by default made me his one and only counselor. We did have two other priesthood holders, both were fourteen years old. They prepared and passed the sacrament, and the two of us blessed it each week. It reminded me of when I was a young priesthood holder. The rest of the branch consisted of about eight women and two or three children.

The Saturday evening before my first block of Sunday meetings, Tomioka informed me that it would be my week to talk in Sacrament Meeting. That was a little rough, to say the least. From that time forward if I wasn't speaking, I conducted the meeting. We rotated these duties each week. I was also the designated chorister for the duration of my stay.

I must admit that my disappointment about not becoming a senior may have affected my attitude towards the work. I suppose I felt that I could be a better senior than my companion; with that, I often felt that we wasted much time during my short forty-two day stay in Hyuga. As I look through my notes we spent a lot of time shopping and looking around. It didn't seem that we worked nearly as hard as we did in my previous places. I have nothing really negative to say about Tomioka Choro; he did a great job with the branch. When we did go out to work, he was a really good missionary and we got a lot done.

I learned more and more about HYOGEN or dialect as my Japanese progressed. My first

Japanese companion, Tomita tried hard to use a more standard form of Japanese, even if he was from Osaka. That was very helpful at the time. On the other hand, Tomioka spoke with a dialect that I hadn't heard before. He was from Tokyo, where one might think that the most standard forms of Japanese are spoken. But this was not the case with Tomioka. Nevertheless, I tried to model my language after his as we worked together.

The mission had only recently instituted a new form of DENDO or proselytizing around the same time I arrived in Hyuga. We called it "Street Dendo". This was simply where missionaries would stand along a sidewalk stopping passersby in their tracks. We would then approach them with a particular Gospel message.

As far as the work went, "Streeting" had to have been the hardest thing that could have been imposed on me. While my Japanese was pretty good, it was in no way spontaneous enough to pull something like this off, or so I thought. Nevertheless, it was our duty to give it a try. But, in my humble opinion, I think that we may have "wasted" hours upon hours doing this. Only about one in every twenty people would even pause to listen to us.

The rules of streeting restricted us to approach only males, unless a female directly approached us. Usually these men would either avoid eye contact, or simply wave their hands in front of their face, as if they were blocking the sun, and say, "I'm too busy".

They didn't even seem to care what our message might be. Additionally, we were further instructed by the Hombu to put together and display a type of flannel board with messages and illustrations to highlight a certain Gospel principle. That quickly went by the wayside, as it only repelled people even further. Of course that may have only been attributed to our terrible artwork.

It wasn't long before Tomioka and I came up with a little game to pass the time. This actually turned out to be a better way to stop people. The rules of the game were simple. When a man approached, one of us would whip open his flip-charts. Today missionaries don't use flip-charts. Simply explained, they were a notebook sized ring binder, with pictures and phrases that matched what you were teaching… flipping them along during the lesson.

Back to the rules of the game… we were never allowed to pre-select any given page; it had to be random. Based on the picture or phrase that appeared, it was our job to come up with an appropriate approach. Anyone who knows anything about those old style flip-charts knows that there was a plethora of options that might appear upon opening a page. Sometimes it might be a picture of Christ or Joseph Smith. Other times you might get words like "The Ten Commandments" or "Eternal Life".

The second and most difficult part of the game was thinking of an appropriate approach for that given page. If a picture of "Jesus" came up, you would basically ask the person if they know who it is, or something simple like that. Stopping people on the street was actually not as hard with this method. Their eyes would fix on the flip-chart and not on my foreign face.

Nevertheless, I became somewhat tentative to do this game after the time when I opened the chart that read "The Law of Chastity". Looking down at it, I was baffled as to how I would approach the man that was now coming towards me. Unexpectedly, he actually stopped as I greeted him. As I began my approach, the only thing that I could think to ask was, "Do you have any daughters?" To my surprise, he did happen to have a teen-aged daughter; and oddly enough, we were able to carry on a very interesting conversation about protecting our children from the temptations of the world and the importance of families.

In a lot of ways, I think that game may have been inspired. I am quite certain that because of our determination in trying to do what we were told, the Spirit gave us the necessary inspiration. We found more and more success using that method over any other one. I soon began to see more of the good missionary in Tomioka as we worked better together over the coming weeks. I realize now that being with him may have been the type of training that I needed at this stage of my mission.

During my first couple of weeks in Hyuga, I also came to realize that my mail hadn't been coming as regular as it should. I was a little down about it; especially since it seemed that much of my time was spent waiting around for my companion to do "Branch business". I was pretty sure that much of that "business" was not necessary for a Missionary/Branch President to have to do, since the overwhelming majority of the already small number of members in Hyuga was female.

In regards to the mail issue; one day, there was a knock on the door. When I opened it, an elderly Caucasian woman stood there. What a surprise that was. During my time in Hyuga, being somewhat of a remote place in Japan, I had the feeling that I was probably the only Caucasian there. It turned out that the woman and her husband (also Caucasian) were Baptist missionaries living there. Her husband's name also happened to be Peter. Since there were probably only two male foreigners in the whole town and both named Peter; without regard to the address, the mailman was apparently taking all the "foreigner named Peter" mail to this other man. This sweet woman handed over all the mail that had been misdirected to them, and then said that she had already informed the mailman to be more careful.

I was so happy to finally get news from home. One of the letters from my dad came as a surprise. It was addressed to "Elder Peter Morris", but the "Elder" was crossed out and replaced with "Uncle". The news of my brother Pat's new baby girl gave me a boost of joy and energy. I was pretty proud to be a brand new uncle. I think I even had a new sense of duty to be a better missionary for my little niece.

Dear Grandma

By now you know that I have moved and also became an uncle. I was really surprised to find out that Bupar had her baby… and also extremely happy. Aren't you?
Today we rode about forty miles on our bikes to do a little sightseeing. It was fun but I sure am worn out. We saw a zoo, a temple, and we also went to the ocean.
Since I'm the only one of about three Americans in the entire city, I'd say that my Japanese is improving a lot. I don't mind that at all.
Like before, I hated to leave, because of all the friends I made. But it wasn't as bad as before. I guess I was used to having to leave. I knew it would come sooner or later…
Take care.

Love Pete

After a week or so in this new area we were awakened by the doorbell. I went down the stairs to find a little boy about seven years old, standing at the doorstep, wearing a little cap and holding a baseball mitt on his hand. "Wanna play catch", he asked pleadingly.

I had never seen this little guy before and now, quite randomly, I am asked to go play ball with him? His innocent look cut me to the core, so without hesitation I ran up and got my P-day clothes on.

It turned out that the elder before me often got up to play with this little boy in front of our house before he went off to school. From that day forward, I continued the tradition. I don't think I ever learned his name, but always referred to him as "Kenji" after a character in one of our missionary films. I enjoyed our little conversations as we played; I actually learned a lot from him. In the process, I grew quite fond of him, as though he was my little brother. This even evoked thoughts and feelings of what kind of a big brother I might have been to my little brother Preston. Would he have been proud to know I was serving my mission?

More often than not, I continued to find myself sitting in the bedroom, waiting for my companion to finish an interview or do some paperwork. I often felt we were wasting precious time. I prayed often for help and guidance. I needed to know that I was doing the right thing and that I was in fact a good missionary. I suppose I was feeling a little sorry for myself. I had an ever growing desire to go senior and could envision taking the lead in getting the work done. I knew I was ready, and continued to wonder why I still hadn't gone senior. I had come to feel very alone.

One particular evening, we were doing a little house-to-house. As we walked the dark streets toward the area where we had planned to work, I felt a strong presence. It felt as though in addition to my companion, someone was with me. This feeling grew stronger as we continued to walk in silence. While it didn't come in the form of a voice, something seemed to tell me that my younger brother may have been permitted to be there with me. Without hearing the actual words, the feeling seemed to say, "I'm serving with you, Pete." I was overcome with a simultaneously chilling and a deeply warm sensation. I don't know how better to explain it, but suddenly, I knew I was not alone anymore.

Whether it was my own imagination or I was really given a special companionship; if only for a moment, I thank my little brother for his support. This was enough to give me a renewed sense of purpose, and it wasn't much longer until I got that call from the Buch.

I was going senior in Kumamoto. Now, as a senior, I felt that I would finally be able to do it "my way". I still have a lot of respect and admiration towards all of my senior companions. I truly know that the Lord put each of them into my life to help me become a stronger, better missionary. Now, for better or worse, it was up to me to show the Lord what I was made of. Ironically, I came to realize that "my way" wasn't my way at all. I soon understood that there would be no success unless we did it the Lord's way.

All in all, Hyuga turned out to be a great transition for me. I'm pretty sure that I may have eaten horse meat for the first time there. I think I may have also gotten the sightseeing bug out of my system there as well. With the possibility of being one of only two Caucasian males in the whole city, I believe that my language skills may very well have doubled.

The sisters in our branch were such an example of faith to me. I began to realize just how much closer and in tune to the spirit woman are in comparison to the average man. With that, I have also come to believe that pride is so much more evident in men than it is in women. Being in Hyuga certainly brought back memories of my younger days at home, performing my priesthood duties week after week. Being one of only two who had the authority to bless the sacrament there, I realized just what a privilege this was. I truly learned to treasure my priesthood in Hyuga.

Chapter 8: Going Senior in Kumamoto

Tomioka Choro and I packed up my things the morning after the transfer call. Sister Watanabe from the branch picked us up in her yellow Mitsubishi Mirage and drove us down to the train station. The rainy season was just beginning, so the train ride was particularly hot and muggy. Every passenger was fanning his or herself with something. As for me, I was basking in my own little private sauna from the inside of my wool-blend suit coat.

Although Kumamoto was to the northwest of Hyuga on the other side of Kyushu Island, there was no direct route across by train. Instead, I was to go northward to the city of Oita, then proceed south, finally heading west to Kumamoto. The whole trip seemed a lot longer than it needed to be.

When I finally arrived, all the missionaries from our area were there. In addition to my new companion, Brown Choro, I was greeted by two Shimai (sisters) and the Zone Leaders or ZLs. One of them was McEntire Choro. Remember him? He was the Hombu secretary that took me out tracting on my second night in Japan. Having a familiar face to greet me made the transition a little easier.

Elder Brown was perhaps a couple of months behind me. Him included, all of my American companions were from Utah. He was a mild mannered sort, yet quite friendly. It wasn't hard to get along with him from the get go. He made me feel very comfortable in my changeover to senior. It didn't take long for us to learn how to work together because as with Hyuga, we already had an appointment for that night. Most days, we managed to keep pretty busy with the investigators that were already established. As I already mentioned, it was the rainy season.

In all my years living in Washington, famous for its wet weather, I don't ever remember the need for an umbrella. Kumamoto had a whole different kind of rain. And because it was also springtime, the temperature rose with every new day. Kumamoto was at the bottom of a basin, creating a natural steam bath effect across the city. We went to the store and bought rain suits in an attempt to keep ourselves dry. Nevertheless, we would end up just as wet on the inside of the suit as the outside from all the humidity. I had never experienced anything like it. In this new area, with all the excitement and activity, I suppose I had neglected a few things.

> Dear Peter,
>
> We haven't received a letter for several weeks but your letter to Grandma explained the reason. I'm glad you are now a senior and I realize that you now have a lot more responsibility and less time.

> I was also happy to hear that you received the pictures. After the birthday package not getting to you, I was afraid the pictures might not either. Your new niece is growing like a weed and getting cuter every day.
>
> We went to Steve's farewell Sunday. It was really nice. I've had a chance to get to know him better since I've been teaching the Sunday School class. I'm sure he's as ready to be as good a missionary as he can be. He read a part of a letter from you to the congregation and I must say, the things you said were exactly what a new missionary needs. I was extremely proud to be your father at that moment, and by the tears that came to Steve, I'm sure he was glad to be your friend.
>
> Please write and let me know how your new assignment is progressing. I hope that in this place you'll get your first baptism. Well I've got to run… write when you can.
>
> Love Dad

From this letter, it would seem that I had been pretty busy. Perhaps I was beginning to gain a similar understanding of the council that was expressed by Gordon B. Hinkley's father when he advised the young Elder Hinkley to "lose yourself and go to work."[27] I'd like to think that was happening to me. I think I was beginning to really understand just why I was in Japan. On the third night in Kumamoto I woke up suddenly to a dream. It was kind of a shock that stirred me; sleep was now out of the question. It was so real to me that I had to get up and write it all down. This is what I wrote in an old unused notebook that someone had left behind:

The dream seemed so real and yet it all made sense. I wonder if it really happened...

There we were all together, one big happy family. You and I were inseparable and always together. We sang together often... those beautiful songs that Father taught us. Life was wonderful and we seemed so very happy. One day, Father called us to come and talk with him. There was already a chill of excitement in the air, because we knew that Father had been planning something wonderful for us. When you and I got there, he asked us both to come and sit with him. Like a flash, I thought of all the other times that we had sat with him. He told us many interesting and exciting stories and we loved to laugh and sing with him. He was never too busy to take us each individually and give us his undivided

---

[27] Quoted in Gordon B. Hinckley, "Taking the Gospel to Britain: A Declaration of Vision, Faith, Courage, and Truth," *Ensign,* July 1987

attention. This time, as we sat with him he seemed a little different. This time he was very serious. In fact, it seemed as though he was going to cry. He began by saying, "My children, I have something very special that I want you to do…" He looked down and continued, "This is very hard for me, but the only way for you to become like me is to do exactly as I tell you." We were a little confused and asked, "What is it Father?" We would do anything for Father. Tears began to well up in his eyes and in his powerful arms; he lifted us both up, holding us close to him.

Father began to reveal his great and wonderful plan to us. He showed us how he had created a new world for us and that it was far away. He went on to say that we were now worthy to go there. On this new world there would be many new things that we could not do with Father. We would also obtain a body much like his. During our time there, we would have to learn those things necessary to become like him someday. His voice began to quiver as he tried to explain what the world would be like when we arrived there. "It will be hard for you… even some of your brothers and sisters will try to hurt and deceive you because of their own confusion and unhappiness." Filled with emotion he went on to say, "You will also experience pain and frustration at times." We found that hard to believe and began to feel sad as well. To comfort us, he told us that there would be many who would know of him and would help us to learn also. He called our brother Jehovah to join us and then reminded us of the sacrifice he will make. He showed us that as Jesus, our Savior, he would pave the way for us to follow. "That is what I ask of you; learn of Him and follow Him!" he said pleadingly. Soon we understood, because we watched and wept as we later saw him suffer for us. He promised that if we would do as he asked, we would be able to return home and live with him forever. Smiles found their way back to our faces.

He then began to give us our assignments in this new world; it would soon be our turn. He told us that because of the special gifts and talents we were given, he had decided where we were to go and what we were to do there. He first turned his attention to me and with a smile said, "I am sending you to a place that is called America. This is a special and choice place. Wonderful things have happened there that have made learning of me more possible than ever before. There I have restored all the things that your brother Jesus provided which are needed to learn and to become like me. You will be given a family and a home where these things are treasured and shared. Your family will love and teach you the way to return to me. They will also teach you how to pray. Through prayer you can come to me with all your questions and problems; I will then be able to better guide and direct you."

Still smiling, he then turned to you, "You I will send to a place that is called

Japan." At first we both became restless at the thought of being separated. Father gently caressed our faces and said, "Please, let me continue…" He explained to you that Japan will be very far from America. But you too would be given a family that will love you. They will teach you to be honest and good. "Alas.", he said "They will not know about me and the Savior, and you will not be taught how to call upon me." Now in tears he added, "But most importantly you will not learn how to come home to me…"

Father turned back to me and said that I wouldn't be going to America because it would be easier, but because he had given me special gifts so that I might share what I had learned to be true; that my testimony would help others to believe as well. He then said that you weren't going to Japan so that it would be difficult, but that Father had instilled in you the ability to endure. You had also been given gifts to be able to recognize the truth when it comes to you. We grew even more afraid that we would lose each other. Just then, Father began to smile.

Father continued by telling us of our missions on earth. He told me first that I would learn many things in America. Most importantly I would learn His true gospel and my role in His great plan. I would know that these things were true, because Father would send a confirmation to my heart so much so that I would want to be a witness of it. My mission was to make my way to Japan and find you. My duty would be to teach you from my heart so that you would understand what your role was in Father's plan.

Your mission was to become an honest and good person. You would be an example to others around you, and your family. "You will be given a special gift, the Light of Christ, your brother", said Father. He told you that with this light you will know what is right and true. Your heart would tell you that something is missing in your life and cause you to wonder if there isn't anything beyond life on Earth. You would have to wait for me to come and find you. When we did find each other, you would have a feeling in your heart that what I would tell you was true. With a smile, Father pointed to me and said, "He will help you to find your way back home to me."

Father embraced us both and sent us away to prepare for our journey. Naturally we were sad at the fact that we would not be together when we arrive to our homes on Earth. But more than that, we were excited to receive our mission calls and hoped that we would be able to live up to Fathers expectations. I loved you even more then. We had grown together, wrapped in the love of our Heavenly Father. As we hugged and said our goodbyes, I sensed a little fear in you. With all confidence, I whispered in your ear, "I will not fail you! I *will* find you! I promise."

Now I am here on Earth. The "veil of my

understanding"[28] has been inconsistent in its translucency. At times my testimony is so strong that I cannot hold back the tears. Yet I have often struggled to understand just why Father sent me here. While I have always known that the gospel is true, it has been easy to forget my purpose in life. Time and again the thoughts of the "Natural Man"[29] cause me to lose track of my real mission. I have come a long way in such a short time.

The knowledge of my savior is an anchor to me. I know that my Father in Heaven lives and has a purpose for me here as a missionary. I sit here at my desk, far from home. The language is hard. The work is exhausting at times. This dream seemed so real and it all actually made sense. I wonder if it really happened. If it is true, than this is it, my moment of truth. Time is running out and I'm half way through my mission here in Japan. Where are you my friend, my dearest friend? How will I know it is you? What if I fail? No! I won't fail! I can't fail! If you really are out there, I will find you. I made a promise to you and ***I will find you.***

I wrote this story that early morning while the others in the apartment slept. The words flowed so very easily because it seemed so real to me. I have kept that old notebook amongst my other mission stuff all these many

[28] D&C 110:1
[29] Mosiah 3:19

years. For a while after that dream, I think I had a sense of renewal to work as hard as I could.

The work in Kumamoto rolled along very quickly. The Japanese language began to flow from my mouth in a way I had never thought it could. Our effectiveness at the doors we knocked on seemed to come with much less effort than I had ever experienced before. Our lessons went more and more like clockwork as the investigators seemed to grasp the concepts more readily.

I know that credit must be given where credit is due. First and foremost, as I recognized then, and can more clearly see now that it was the Spirit of the Lord that was with us. As we exerted more and more effort, the Lord in turn increased his aid. I can't deny that fact. Secondly, I had a humble and good hearted companion whose heart was one with mine in the work. We were so busy and could see the effects of our labors every day.

The other missionaries we worked with in this area were also an inspiration. The ZLs, McEntire Choro and Iino Choro, were a joy to be around. We would sing every chance we could. If there's anything I remember about Iino Choro it would have to be his strong testimony and his beautiful voice. Together, the ZLs were very capable missionaries.

On the fifth Sunday in Kumamoto, we had a baptismal meeting. This would have been only the second baptism I had had the privilege of attending thus far. Sundays were the best day to do them, because we would always have a good turnout by the members. This baptism was for a young man, Brother Horiguchi, whom the zone leaders had been teaching. I remember how excited he was on that day. We were all excited.

While I stood at the back of the room watching the baptismal ordinance, I noticed an unfamiliar young man in the room. He was noticeable because he was wearing the uniform of a gas station attendant. He stood and watched the baptism alongside the rest of us. As we had never seen him before, we introduced ourselves. He pointed in the direction of the font, and referring to the baptism that he had just witnessed said, "That's what I want".

It turned out that the young man worked at a nearby gas station. He had noticed the cars and numbers of people that came to church each Sunday. That particular day, he had a strong impression to finally look inside. I am sure that the Spirit bore witness to him as he watched Brother Horiguchi enter the waters of baptism. I don't know what ever happened to that young man. But it was exciting to see the Spirit guide him, and cause him to recognize the necessity of the ordinance of baptism.

As we worked hard together, my companion and I began to see success just around the corner. I was sure that we were only a couple of steps away from getting our first baptisms. We were teaching a very wonderful family, the Yamaguchi family. Mr. Yamaguchi's work had him travel on occasion. On our first visit, I noticed on the lapel of his suit jacket was an Angel Moroni pin. He explained that he acquired it when he had gone to New York for work and was invited to an outdoor performance.

I would venture to guess that Mr. Yamaguchi's host was LDS, because the more he described this show, it became apparent that he had gone to see the Hill Comorah pageant in New York. He said that it was very entertaining, but didn't understand much of it. Mr. and Mrs. Yamaguchi showed an interest in the concepts of the gospel very quickly. It seemed as though our lessons could have come straight out of a missionary training video or something. Their questions flowed as if they were reading a script. Chills literally ran down my spine when out of the blue they began asking about the baptismal ordinance. This of course opened the discussion regarding the necessity of baptism by immersion. Thus far in my mission, I had never gotten this far with an investigator. I was certain that they would soon be baptized. The baptism of an entire family was a rare thing, and I really thought we had one in our back pocket here.

There were a few other investigators that were making progress as well. A very active young sister approached me at church one Sunday. Sister Inada, the only member in her family, invited us to come and teach at her house. Her mother, brother, and a cousin had become interested in learning about the gospel. As we taught them, a special spirit abounded as Sister Inada bore her testimony alongside ours. As we progressed with the lessons, the feeling to challenge them to be baptized regularly crept into my mind. I only wish I would have acted on that prompting; I was sure that in a very short time and with just a little more effort, Sister Inada's family as well as the Yamaguchi family would be baptized.

As it would turn out, I only ended up staying in Kumamoto for thirty-five days. I was shocked and crushed as the Buch explained the transfer over the phone. I would be traveling a short train ride northward to the small city of Omuta. I was in the midst of my greatest success as a missionary thus far. I think I even saw the impending baptisms in my sleep. If such a thing is possible, I could almost taste them. All I could say to myself was that I was robbed. My heart ached. The other three missionaries in the apartment tried to console me, but I couldn't shake the twinge of antagonism that I had towards whatever it was that caused this tragedy to happen.

I was at a loss as to who to direct my frustration towards. It was extremely difficult to see the logic in sending me away when so much good was happening. I suppose that I just needed to default to the old adage, "The Lord Works in Mysterious Ways". It would be a little while for me to see it, but the answer did come in Omuta.

Perhaps the Lord offered me a little comfort later that evening. After a day of running around to say goodbye to the many people whom I had come to know in such a short time, I received a phone call from Sister Koga. Remember her, back in Futsukaichi? Stoneman and I watched the Super Bowl at her house. I don't really know, even to this day, how she knew I was transferring, much less that I was going to Omuta. But she called to tell me that Brother Koga's mother lived in Omuta and that they happened to be visiting there the next day. They would arrange to come and see me at my new apartment once I arrived.

Just knowing that there would be familiar faces waiting to see me on transfer day seemed to put my heart a little more at ease. It was hard to say goodbye to McEntire in particular. He turned out to be a pretty good friend. Brown would be going senior with a green-bean and of course I was happy for him. I encouraged him to be bold and not to wait in challenging the Inada and Yamaguchi families. Later Brown reported that neither of them had accepted the challenges at that time. Who can say whether my staying might have made a difference; I can only pray that they made it later on down the line.

Chapter 9: Omuta, My Home in Japan

On the morning of transfers, we made our way down to the station. Brown's greenie had arrived on time, so together we all carried my stuff to the train. Sister Inada's mother and cousin came to see me off. It was hard to hold back the tears as they said their goodbyes in the form of sobs. In a way, I felt like I was abandoning them as I stepped onto that train. The ride itself was only a little over forty-five minutes.

I would be working with yet another Japanese companion, Nishino Choro. It was a pretty rare thing to get so many Japanese companions; so far I was batting 500, 3 out of 6. Nishino had a good handle on the area and the investigators, so we didn't waste any time when I got there. After riding around all day meeting a few of our investigators, we headed for home just in time to get a phone call from Brother and Sister Koga. They were already in town and wanted to come up to the apartment. When they arrived, I was so happy to see them; it was kind of like coming home. They brought me a hefty supply of groceries and other special goodies. Thanks to the Kogas, my transfer day was a little less painful.

Dear Grandma,

You'll never believe it, but I've transferred again. Now I'm about an

hour north of where I just was and about an hour south of where I was in January thru March. It's called Omuta. I was really upset to move again. I hate it! I made so many friends in my last place.
Now I have another Japanese companion. He's only been out for three months. He's a real fun little chubby Japanese fellow. I like him.
I love Japan so much! If you ever get the urge to go, let me know. I'll take you around, for sure! It's the greatest place in the world. I just know I'll want to come back here as soon as I can.
I love you and think of you all the time. Take care.

Love Pete

There were two other elders with us in the apartment at Omuta; Callister Choro, yet another elder from Utah. His companion was Yamada Choro. I liked him from the very start. He always had a smile on his face and carried with him a very strong testimony. Right away, I could see that my new companion, Nishino Choro seemed a little distracted as we worked. I knew that he wanted to go senior because he said as much all the time. I began to understand what I must have sounded like just a couple of months earlier.

Aside from his tremendous snoring,

Nishino was a pretty good companion. But oh my, the snoring; his snoring was so loud that the floor literally shook beneath us. I tried everything I could think of to quiet him. I rolled him over, called out to him, and even threw small objects at him. I soon realized that I was so busy at night trying to overcome his snoring that I was hardly getting any sleep myself. One night, I suppose I couldn't bear another sleepless night, so without thinking, I wadded a sock into a ball and inserted it into his mouth as it opened. Suffice it to say, he was not pleased.

The enraged Elder Nishino suddenly awoke and began telling me what a mean and cruel thing I had just done. If it's any consolation, to the best of my recollection it was a sock from my clean laundry; throughout my apology I carefully tried to explain how distracting his snoring had been and how I was losing sleep. Let's just say, I wasn't able to convince him of my plight, so I ended up opening the sliding glass door to our balcony, which was already on my side of the room. I opened it just wide enough to lay my head on a pillow outside. I continued to sleep like that the rest of the time that I was with Nishino. Fortunately, it was only one month.

I had already mentioned Omuta at the beginning of this story. In comparison to all the other areas where I had served, Omuta covered the most territory. Nevertheless, we only had a handful of active investigators when I arrived; I will name a few. On the very first day we visited Hirakawa-san. My first impression of her was that she liked the company of the missionaries, if only for the entertainment value. She was a stay-at-home mom with a two and a half year old daughter and a set of twin baby boys. Next we had the Matsunaga Family.

Actually it was Mrs. Matsunaga and her four kids. I never was able to meet the husband. It didn't take long for me to fall in love with those kids. Mrs. Matsunaga had been introduced to the missionaries by Sister Hiroshima. Sister Hiroshima had only been a member for a short time herself, and was a great help in fellowshipping the Matsunagas. We also visited Mori-san.

Mori-san was a young man, maybe twenty-two or three. He was a part time bass player in a band. We usually taught him along with his girlfriend at his parent's house. On the third day we met Muramoto-san, the librarian. Because he lived so far away, we would meet him at the library and he would drive us out to his house. He liked to have us over so we could listen and comment on his philosophies regarding life and religion… while we tried to work in a lesson.

Finally, Sister Murata from the branch had long struggled to have the missionaries over to teach her husband. If we ever did meet with him it was pretty much only to appease her. During the next few weeks with Nishino Choro, we spent most days toggling between these houses and the homes of some of the members.

At first, the days seemed very monotonous in Omuta. I suppose I was still jaded with thoughts of my previous area. I really had a grip on the situation there. So with this banishment to Omuta, it sometimes felt like I was merely babysitting some other missionaries' old and seemingly stagnant investigator pool. It's not to say that we didn't have any progress at all. Within a week of my arrival, I managed to get Hirakawa-san to quit smoking. I still have her last pack of cigarettes in a box somewhere. Obviously we had been teaching her the Word of Wisdom lesson and I challenged her to give up smoking and coffee. In return, I would make a pact with her. If she managed to quit smoking for a week, I would eat a package of my most feared food in Japan, Natto.

In short, natto is fermented soy beans. The process for making natto is to introduce a bacterium, administer constant heat for a day, and then let it sit a week to age. The result is beans in a stringy, molasses like consistency with a strong odor. To me the aroma was actually a little offensive.

Growing up in Washington State, I usually worked in the vegetable fields during the summer. From about the 4th grade, I started by picking strawberries; and the following summers I moved on to rogueing spinach, picking cucumbers, and finally driving a pea-viner combine after getting my license. The only bathrooms available in those fields were porta-potties or rather, simple outhouses. Anyone who has ever had the experience knows the distinctive smell of such a place. Needless to say, I found it once again with natto.

I don't mean to offend anyone who likes natto, but that's the way I smelled it. The following week when Hirakawa-san reported her abstinence from tobacco, an unopened pack of cigarettes and a pack of natto were waiting on the table just for me. It was all I could do to keep it inside me for the rest of the day. To add insult to injury, I was compelled to give her a box of candy which was sent from home, in appreciation for her keeping her word. A couple of weeks later, she even quit coffee as well; this time without any strings attached.

> Dear Peter,
>
> I got your letter a couple of days ago and thought I would answer it now. I just wrote to Steve. I guess he will be leaving for Hong Kong very soon now.
> You really sound like you are putting your "all" into your mission, with the long hours you spend. It seems when we are doing the Lord's work time indeed goes by fast. I remember when I was doing missionary work. One night we had 3 cottage meetings (one was your dad's). He came to my house

so that made it a little easier. But after his meeting we had two other ones. It was after 10:30 before we got home. It was well worth it though and I didn't even feel tired...
I was proud to hear you are teaching your investigators the Word of Wisdom. But to have to use the means that you did sure took a lot of intestinal fortitude. Fermented beans I am afraid would not be my best selection either. She really did want to test your mettle. She must have been quite nice though to give you socks and handkerchiefs. Take good care of yourself.

Love Grandma

In spite my little victory with Hirakawa-san, over those first three weeks, my feelings and attitude towards what we were (or perhaps were not) getting accomplished grew more and more dark. It seemed that we were plodding along in a rut, doing the same thing day after day and seeing only the tiniest of results. Of course I know now that in reality we were doing much more. But I was anxious to move the work along and found it hard to see any progress. We would go around to the above mentioned homes sometimes just shooting the breeze, or so it seemed. We also knocked on door after door with little or no results.

I can't be sure what was happening

during this time, but we were even finding it hard to make appointments with the investigators that we did have. I was really getting frustrated. Not long after the natto incident, I began looking through the area book in our apartment thinking I might be able to resurrect an old or perhaps dormant investigator that hadn't been contacted for a while.

Most of the entries in this book explained why the missionaries had stopped going. Usually the reason was that the investigators had clearly declined any further contact. I left nearly all of those alone. But there was one page in the book that I repeatedly passed over due to what was boldly written diagonally across it, "DROPPED". It seemed clear that we needn't bother with that one. Yet due to the lack of any other possibilities, I paused briefly to read the details. Not long before me, one my predecessors had made the decision not to visit the Umezawa family, writing comments such as, they are "not responsive" to the lessons or they were "uncooperative".

My original feeling was to skip the Umezawas altogether. But the more I dwelled on it, the more curious I became; it was never actually stated that they didn't want any further contact with the missionaries; so I decided that we should at least check it out for ourselves. We made it a regular practice to stop at the Umezawa's house whenever we passed through their area… although each time, no one ever seemed to be home. It would be weeks before we would ever make any contact with them. Somehow I sensed that this was going to be a challenge.

My frustration finally hit its peak on one particular day as our routine had become more and more tedious. Early one day we taught Mori-san (the electric bass player) and his girlfriend lesson number two. It felt like we were only going through the motions with him; almost like the lessons were just an excuse to hang out there. The rest of the day didn't seem to get any better. We had an appointment with Hirakawa-san, but when we arrived; her little girl informed us that her mommy was taking a bath. By default, we ended up going down the street to Sister Hiroshima's house. She was very kind to make us dinner before our next appointment with Sister Murata's husband.

When we arrived at the appointment, Sister Murata met us at the door only to tell us that her husband had drunk a few beers after dinner and had fallen asleep on the floor in front of the TV. Of course, she apologized, but we found ourselves with nothing left to do that evening. I suppose I had reached the extent of my frustration. At that moment, it was as if I was in a train on a track. It felt as though someone or something had thrown a switch that sent this train into a direction that I wasn't prepared to go. Or perhaps the switch led to a turnout where the train seemed to slow to an eventual stop. I guess I felt I was being unduly punished; yet believed that I was trying hard to be a good missionary.

Leaving Sister Murata's house, Nishino Choro looked at his watch and suggested that there wasn't enough time to do anymore. "Let's just call it a day", he said in so many Japanese words. With no alternative plan of my own, my head started to nod as we mounted our bikes. Riding down the street, staring at the back of my companion; the feeling of failure seemed to ebb up inside of me. I was sure that it was only going to get worse. Fortunately with Nishino in front of me, he couldn't see the streaks on my cheeks that the tears were making as the wind blew on my face. I prayed, "Lord, what am I doing wrong? I try to follow the rules; I get up on time; I study. What on earth am I doing wrong?"

As I tried to focus through the blurry lenses of my eyes, I believe I received an answer of sorts. "Try a little harder" was the feeling that resonated in my head. Without thinking, I hollered for Nishino to come back. We came together in front of a street that led into another neighborhood. "Let's do some house to house" I blurted out. He had a puzzled look on his face. Still not understanding where this idea had come from, I told my companion that we would only have to knock on two doors, one for each of us.

We agreed that if, with these two doors, we didn't find anyone; we could go home. Maybe I was trying to put faith to the test like Alma or Ammon. But truthfully, I didn't know what I was trying to pull off. But I suppose I did have hopes for a miracle. Nishino just shrugged his shoulders as we parked our bikes on the corner. Utilizing the all determining "rock-paper-scissors", it was decided that Nishino would go first.

Both of our doors were opened by women. We approached both doors in the usual fashion, "Is your husband home?" Traditionally, it wasn't a good idea for elders to contact housewives without the husband at home, unless they invited us in. Nishino's new "potential" contact said that her husband was in the bathtub. Like most other times before, we excused ourselves and promised to come back again another time (which we usually didn't end up doing). My contact on the other hand, said that her husband hadn't returned from work.

Well there it was, perhaps the answer to my prayer. I didn't know what I was looking for, as far as miracles go, but this certainly wasn't it. As with the first house, I politely excused myself with the same promise to return; the kind young housewife slowly closed the door. I don't know how obvious it was but I'm pretty sure I was trudging away in disappointment… or perhaps shame. Just then, we heard the door open again and the woman called out, "Are you missionaries?" My heart skipped a beat as we shuffled back to the doorway again.

The woman's name was Yamashita-san. She proceeded to tell the story of how some years ago in high school; a friend invited her to an English class at a church. Missionaries like us were the teachers of the class. By her description, it seemed as though English was kind of the side subject of the class's purpose. They showed a film about Jesus and then gave out books to everyone. She continued to say that it was very uncomfortable for her, so she never went back. She then excused herself for a moment, bringing back her Japanese version of *The Book of Mormon*. For some reason, without ever even opening it, she had kept it on her bookshelf all these years.

There at the door, I had the opportunity to teach Yamashita-san a little about the book and then gave a short testimony of its truth. I asked her if we could come back and talk more. She hesitated, saying that she wasn't sure if it would be a good idea. I then asked her if she was still interested in learning English. She smiled and nodded her head. I assured her that at our English class, we only taught English. Ironically, it has become Church policy for missionaries in Japan to refrain from combining English lessons with Gospel lessons. It has become a free public service rather than a means of finding investigators. Of course if one of the students should ask, the missionaries are more than happy to make an appointment to meet at another time.

So with a little extra prodding, Mrs. Yamashita agreed to come to our class, if she could find the time. For some reason, my heart was at ease. Was this my answer? Actually, it didn't matter, because I went home with the feeling that something had actually happened that night.

I still have a difficult time fully understanding what happened with Yamashita-san. On the surface it would have seemed like a simple happy turn of events. We found a person that happened to have a *Book of Mormon* and wanted to come to our English class. Perhaps to many missionaries, this could have been an everyday event. But for me, this was just the boost I was hoping for; I felt so much better. To me it was like shifting gears, or perhaps the beginning of a new chapter.

Two days after finding Yamashita-san, we had a breakthrough with Mori-san. After numerous invitations, he finally offered a prayer for the first time. With that, my heart began to swell bigger and bigger each day. It was the day after Mori-san's prayer that we gave Yuka the *Plan of Salvation* pamphlet. At the beginning of this narrative, I related the story of Yuka, the girl in our English class who asked "So, what is it that you guys really do all day, besides teaching English?" Yuka's long journey began that very day.

Interestingly enough, a couple of weeks later Yamashita-san (the lady with *The Book of Mormon*) showed up at our English class. When the class had finished, she asked the very same question that Yuka had asked, "So, what is it that you guys really do all day, besides teaching English?" We were finally beginning to see things fall in to place as we sat there in that little branch building (actually it was a house). Yamashita-san listened intently as we taught her the first discussion.

About this same time, Nishino Choro transferred out of Omuta. My new companion was yet another Japanese elder, Nakamura Choro. Nearly instantaneously my new companion joined the fraternity of my most favorite companions. I will never forget his humility. Although he was nearly four years older, he displayed an enormous level of respect for me as his senior companion. It didn't take long for me to develop a real love for him. It was very hard for any of us in the apartment to be mad at him despite his chronic clumsiness.

Our bath area had a white tile floor. Next to the bathtub was a sink where we all brushed our teeth. I can recall on more than one occasion when Nakamura Choro dropped and broke a glass on that tile floor. Sweep and rinse all you want, but that clear glass blended into the tile floor so well that we had to wear flip-flops when we bathed for days after.

Each week, time was set aside for each companion set to go over that week's appointments and to evaluate one another. At the conclusion of the meeting, each companion would have the opportunity to comment on how they felt about anything regarding the work… or even about each other.

Never did I ever hear a single complaint or a word of criticism come from Nakamura

Choro's mouth, with only one exception. He simply asked me to slow down on the bikes. Apparently, with the excitement of the work and all our appointments, we became so busy that we hardly had any time to take a rest. I should have been more aware of this. At that moment I realized how much I had literally been dragging poor Nakamura Choro around that humongous area. Yet regrettably, I don't know if I ever considered how he felt. Actually, his comment came in the aftermath of a small bike incident. To this day I have never seen anyone do a summersault with a bicycle, either before or since I saw Elder Nakamura accomplish it.

Summer in Omuta was extremely hot, and so was the work. We worked harder than any other place I had been. The only break we did take was for a conference where Elder William Bradford of the Seventy came and spoke to us. At the beginning of July that year, the Church had created thirteen administrative areas around the world. Elder Bradford was assigned to be the area president in Asia.

To be honest, I don't think many of us were excited to hear his message… once he got started. Elder Bradford, who also served his mission in Japan back in the early fifties, clearly had an interest in the missionary work there. With visual aids, he proceeded to tell us how our mission had the worst numbers of any other Asian mission. Naturally for many of us, this criticism was hard to swallow.

Elder Bradford proceeded to tell us that

we simply weren't finding enough people to teach. He even went so far as to say that he himself could go out for a morning jog, on any given day, in any area, and gather enough appointments to last him the rest of the day and into the evening. Of course that prompted a lot of whispering in that chapel. Meaning no disrespect of course, my own first thought was, "Okay Elder, come on over to Omuta and show us how it's done." I know that I probably should have become humbled, taking his words to heart. But in my mind, we were already on fire at the moment. I sort of felt like he was some number-crunching general, who sits at the back of the battle, looking at the front lines through binoculars.

Did I absolutely miss the point or what? Elder Bradford was unquestionably right, and I was wrong in so many ways. On the train ride home and for the next few days, we had several opportunities to discuss and ponder upon Elder Bradford's instruction. Eventually, the four of us broke down and decided to put his challenge to the test. Equipped with pamphlets in the pockets of our sweat pants, we went out for a jog.

That morning, aside from the occasional salary man in a rush, the only people up and about in the wee hours of the morning were elderly people. Many were gathered at the community park. They were smart to take advantage of the cool morning air either to walk, do Tai Chi, or play Gate Ball (Croquet). Although we weren't exactly able to rack up enough appointments to last us into the night, we did manage to strike up some good conversation with a few of these wonderful people.

If anything, I learned my lesson and quickly developed a deep respect for what Elder Bradford was trying to relate to us. He was merely saying what I had already heard not too long before: "Try a little harder". Nakamura Choro and I decided that we probably could work a little harder.

Not long after finding our new found zeal, I had an interview with the Buch at a zone conference. As usual, he asked what my number goals looked like for the upcoming month. Perhaps in the wake of our enthusiasm, I tossed out a seemingly ridiculous goal. For some reason, I blurted out that we would raise our teaching pool to twenty-five units. At that point, we only had about ten. This meant that we would need to find, and begin teaching another fifteen… in a single month. That was almost unheard of in our mission. I think a more reasonable mission-wide average was maybe four or five. The Buch chuckled a little, patted me on the back, and then sent me on my way.

When I told Nakamura our new goal, true to his humble nature, he simply took a big gulp and suggested that we go to work right away. That month, our days were long and hard. Most of the time, we scarcely had a moment even for the tiniest of breaks. Looking at one of my day planner entries:

Friday, August 10
Up, studied and got ready. Big plans. Went out and tried to find Brother Moro. Went to the Nakazono's house. Came back to rest for a minute (HOT). Got slides and went to Kajihara's house… showed film (good). Went to Mori's… showed film (great talk). Burned over to Yuka's house (talked and showed film). Back for 10 minute rest then went to Eto-san's house (lesson and film). Came back… Real tired. Bed.

I don't know what the deal was with all the film showing that particular day. But I guess if you're going to haul that bulky projector around, you might as well make the most of it. But the point is that we were very busy. In case you weren't counting, we had six lessons that day covering perhaps 50 square miles. The exhaustion was actually exhilarating. We could truly feel the blessings pouring from Heaven's windows. Believe it or not, we found Hatazoe-san, our number twenty-five, on our way back from the Umezawa's house at about 9:30pm on the last day of the month.

On the way back to the apartment, I suppose we were feeling a little down about being so close to our goal and falling just one shy of it. I had resolved to the fact that it was simply too late to knock on any more doors that night. It was actually Nakamura Choro, who posed the argument that it was still early enough to get even just a tiny bit of tracting in. This would be one of those rare times when Nakamura would exert his opinion so strongly; so with that, we turned into an apartment complex along the way.

Looking up at the building, I suggested that we only do one row of doors on the first staircase. This gave us eight doors to find one new contact; on top of that, we had to make an appointment. We took turns at the doors, starting with Nakamura. On the third door, Nakamura wasn't getting very far with a particular young man and we were just about to turn and leave. Without fully understanding why, I felt somewhat impressed to at least give this man my card.

Most missionaries in Japan carried business cards with mission home and personal information. Japanese people are accustomed to such a practice. I believe that perhaps my particular card was a little unique in comparison to many of the other cards I saw missionaries give out. Back in Kumamoto, Elder McEntire and I had our cards made at the prefectural penitentiary.

As it was with license plate manufacturing at prisons in the States, apparently some Japanese prisons made business cards. Along with the standard mission information and my name, I simply added a short phrase, "Shindara doko ni iku… kana?" In English this means something like, "I wonder where we go when we die…" This simple, yet profound question often intrigued people when they read it.

That night, Hatazoe-san read the phrase out loud and chuckled. As with many times before, I followed up with something like, "Do you have an answer for that?" He answered with a shrug. I continued, "What would you say if I told you that I knew the answer?" By his puzzled grin, I sensed his curiosity so I asked if we might come back and explain. He agreed, and we made an appointment to come and teach him about the Plan of Salvation. We tried to contain ourselves as we quietly made our way down the stairs to our bikes. All the way back to the apartment we cheered and hollered. I had never seen the mild mannered Elder Nakamura being so noisy.

As I mentioned, that night we were on our way back from the Umezawa's house. If you recall, the Umezawa's had been recorded as "DROPPED" in the area book. We had been religiously (no pun intended) trying to contact them each time we passed their neighborhood over the course of many weeks. Sometimes, someone would be home. But as we were greeted through the door, the reply was always, "now is not a good time". We never saw anything of them except through the opaque glass of the front door. Finally after weeks of doing this, we managed to catch Mr. Umezawa outside the house one afternoon. To my eternal surprise he greeted us with, "Where have you been all this time?" I didn't know how to respond as he began to tell me how it had all worked before.

If the missionaries wanted to visit the Umezawas, it would have to be according to the work schedule of their twenty-year-old daughter, Chiyo. We could only visit them if she was available. In his voice was the hint that his daughter may not be very excited to see us. But after our short visit, he seemed to like us and told me to call the following Wednesday evening. He went on to say that Chiyo was sure to be home and that he would help to arrange an appointment.

We did as Mr. Umezawa instructed and I placed the call. Over the phone, I could hear Mr. Umezawa with his hand somewhat muffling the receiver, "It's the missionaries; they want to come over; how about tomorrow night?" I could then hear Chiyo's reply, "Tell them I'm not going to be home" He then spoke into the receiver and said, "Come on over tomorrow, we'll all be home." With Chiyo still protesting in the background, I heard him hang up.

That following evening we rode our bikes to the Umezawa home. To my surprise, Chiyo pleasantly greeted us at the door and then let us in. After ushering us into the living room, she politely excused herself saying that she had work to do in the other room. So we spent a good part of that evening… with her parents. We enjoyed a pleasant conversation where they explained that they only felt comfortable speaking about "churchy stuff" if Chiyo were present. This of course scaled down the conversation to what added up to merely a casual chit-chat. After a while of this, I suggested that we come back again, when Chiyo wasn't so busy. Chiyo's mother called her into the room.

When Chiyo eventually joined us in the living room, I stated that we only wanted to get to know them. We simply wanted to come back to introduce ourselves better. She seemed to be open to that sort of meeting, but in the same breath said that it was a very busy time. I responded that our schedule was wide open and we could adjust our time to her schedule.

What happened next took me somewhat by surprise. I almost flipped out when she walked over to the calendar on the wall and began turning the pages while saying, "This month is no good; I'm still busy this next month too…" She probably would have continued with each calendar page until there were no more pages to turn. Somewhat frustrated, I interrupted this little display of her "extremely busy schedule" to suggest that we could just come by another time; and if they weren't particularly busy, we could meet again. Chiyo and I promised to make no promises.

From the time that we began trying to contact the Umezawa Family to the time that we were finally teaching them, I was able to see an entire INASAKU (rice crop) season. Farmers had already planted the little SANAE (rice seedlings) in the shin-deep mud by the time we started. During the weeks of trying to get

Chiyo to open the door again, some of the farmers were starting INEKARI (reaping rice).

I refer to that because on the way back from another lesson, way out in the countryside, I realized that I had never seen a stalk of rice up close. I had seen nearly any other type of crop, but rice was a new one for me. We made a stop just long enough for me to break off a small bunch of rice stalks. I know that was wrong, but I promise it was only a few stalks. I thought I might press them in a book or something.

With nowhere to store the rice stalks, I had to hold them in my hand as we once again took our chances at the Umezawa's door. I had grown accustomed to the voice of Chiyo, telling us that they were busy; I of course, expected to hear as much again this time. But just after I knocked, looking down at my lovely golden rice stalks, I felt prompted to change my door approach. So when Chiyo asked, "Who's there?" My mouth took over and said, "Rice delivery."

It was fairly common for families to have bags of rice delivered to their doorstep, seeing that it is the staple diet of Japan. Chiyo replied, "Who?" Once again I repeated "Rice delivery?" I began wondering what the heck I was doing, and judging from his expression, so was my companion.

Surprisingly, Chiyo stepped down to the genkan and opened up the door, only to see my slightly embarrassed face. I presented the baby bushel of rice and said once again, "Rice delivery?" She began laughing out loud and motioned for us to come inside. With this somewhat slow start, we actually began teaching the Umezawa's the lessons. Well, in truth we only taught Chiyo and her mom, while her dad watched TV.

With the Umezawas on the list, we continued teaching our now very large pool of investigators. I even felt that a number of them were coming very close to being baptized. Over this period of time, the other Elders in the apartment managed to schedule a baptism of their own.

As we had been teaching Yamishita-san, we invited her to the baptism. By this time, we had gone through all the lessons and she had even come to church a few times. Only four days earlier, I had challenged her to be baptized. Nevertheless, she was a little worried about what her family; or rather her husband's family would do if she were to join. Attending this baptism helped her to make up her mind. My heart was full as I had the privilege of witnessing her mighty change[30].

Yamashita-san called me that evening, tearfully expressing that she wanted baptism for herself. She received an interview the following Thursday, and on Sunday, I was blessed to take that wonderful sister into the waters of baptism. Following the baptism, Nakamura Choro conferred her as the newest member of the Church. I had fasted from Friday

[30] Alma 5:14

to Sunday in the hopes that Yamashita-san, and any of our other investigators who were coming, would feel the Spirit and the truthfulness of what she was embarking on.

It was tradition to have baptisms on Sundays after Church. As I mentioned before, most people had Sunday off and we stood a better chance of member attendance. Following the baptism, it was also tradition that the baptized person stand and offers a brief testimony. All in attendance were overcome by the strong and sweet spirit. When Sister Yamashita bore her testimony, there wasn't a dry eye in that tiny chapel. I could hardly contain myself either, as tears soaked the front of my white shirt.

Dear Pete,

I hope your baptism went as planned and that the Church is a little larger because of it. Like they always say, they are only statistics and aren't that important. If that's so, why are the leaders always talking statistics? Anyway, I hope things are going well with you.
All is going well here. Pat says you owe him a letter. We see our baby about twice a week and I'm doing a wonderful job of spoiling her.
Your dog King says "hi" and wishes you'd come home soon. We love you.
Until next time.

Love Dad

Not long after that, my mom sent a letter telling me that she had received a letter from Yamashita-san. Mom said she broke down in tears as Yamashita-san bore her testimony to my parents. She began by thanking them for making it possible to send me to Japan so that I could find her and bring the Gospel to her. Of course, I was not aware that Yamashita-san had done such a thing and was surprised to hear about it from Mom. I was really feeling good at this point of my mission. That baptism only fueled our burning enthusiasm. More and more opportunities to teach the gospel to the people of Omuta became available.

The power and inspiration of the Lord increased as we tried to work to the best of our ability. Some of the experiences from that time are still very special and sacred to me. I have already mentioned the Matsunaga family. We often visited the mom and her four kids. Our lesson progression was set at a very slow pace. I fell in love with those adorable children of hers, particularly the younger two. We made it a point to visit their house whenever we passed that way.

We tried to plan our visits around Matsunaga-san's work schedule so we could catch her at home. They always seemed so excited whenever we stopped by. The little ones made us feel like their big brothers. Nevertheless, on one particular day as we entered the house, things seemed out of the ordinary. The mother wasn't home yet, but the kids invited us in. Gradually, something began to feel very strange; I struggled to put my finger on what it was, and I could sense that Nakamura Choro was feeling the same way.

As we sat there, certain clues to this strangeness began to unravel. Firstly, as it was the middle of the summer, it seemed odd that the electric fan wasn't running. As always, the kids offered us something cool to drink from the fridge. Yet from where the two of us were sitting, we could see that the only thing in the fridge was the pitcher of wheat tea. It became clear to us that something was terribly wrong. The younger kids were as cheerful as ever, but the older two seemed a little distant. When the phone rang, they all ignored it as if it was wrong to answer it. The mood grew more and more mysterious.

After a short while, Matsunaga-san came home from work. She seemed a little surprised to see us; almost embarrassed that we were in her house. In a very uncharacteristic fashion, she politely asked us to leave. Upon leaving, we headed straight to Sister Hiroshima's house to see if she could help us understand what might have been wrong. As she and Matsunaga-san were good friends, we thought she might have some information.

Sister Hiroshima told us that she was aware that Matsunaga-san's husband had gambled away a good portion of his monthly paycheck. It seemed clear that they had run out of money.

We further assumed that from what we saw or rather didn't see in the fridge meant that they were not even able to buy groceries. As we rode home, both of us felt that something needed to be done. Without much discussion, we decided to at least go to the store and buy them some groceries.

At the grocery store, we realized that our money supply was sorely lacking. Nevertheless, we gathered as much of the basics as we could. We began to feel a little guilty at the meager amount we were able to assemble as we started to head for the check out. Just then, and seemingly by chance, the other elders walked into the store. Without even asking the details, they both handed over whatever money they had in their pockets. This allowed us to buy rice and milk, in addition to what we already had. The problem now, was how to give it to them without embarrassing Matsunaga-san.

We decided on the good old American way of taking the goods to the doorstep, knocking on the door, and then running away. As we hid in the bushes, we watched dear Matsunaga-san look around to see who had left the bags. We crouched down so as not to be spotted. She then scooped up the bags and went inside. Just as we started to stand up to go, her door opened up again. We quietly looked on as Matsunaga-san carried one of the bags to the adjoining house where an elderly lady lived. Prior to seeing that, I was feeling pretty good about the little sacrifice we thought we had made. But this quickly paled in comparison to Matsunaga-san's act of kindness. I certainly learned a great lesson of humility that day.

Among everything else that was going on, we had been charged with the task of teaching a little girl in the branch. Being slightly over the age of eight, it had become necessary to go through the lesson plan with little Sakiko Tokunaga. Upon completion, I had the most wonderful opportunity of baptizing her as well. I was reminded of that blustery day in October each time I have had the privilege to baptize my own children.

I should mention the procedure we had to go through in order to have a baptism in Omuta. Obviously, the house where we held our branch meetings was not equipped with a font. We nevertheless managed to make do with something between a small pool and a giant bathtub. This "font" was located in the garden area next to the building. The elders would come early to church and fill it about two-thirds of the way full with the garden hose. After the block of meetings, we boiled large pots of water on the stove. In an attempt to take the chill off the freezing water, the hot water was added at the last minute.

Sakiko's mother was so happy and proud. I truly felt like her big brother as I climbed on a chair to get into the font with Sakiko's little arms wrapped around my neck. As it was with Yamashita-san, tears streamed down my cheeks as I recited the baptismal prayer. And just like Yamashita-san (now Yamashita-shimai or *Sister* Yamashita) little Sakiko also bore her testimony. I was so impressed to see this young little sister speak with such clarity and emotion. I think her mother's tears came from the relief of seeing her little girl take this important step in her life, in spite of the fact that Sakiko's dad wasn't a member.

Perhaps the best part of that day was the several investigators who had come to attend Sakiko's big day. Chiyo Umezawa and her mom came. Watanabe-san, a nurse we met at the hospital when I got a sinus infection, also came. Even when my head felt like it was about to blow up, the Lord saw fit to lead us to the right place at the right time. Kunisaki-san, Moro-san, and even Honda-san came. I suppose this might be an appropriate time to tell you how we found Honda-san.

Sometime before Sakiko's baptism, the Buch decided to make me the District Leader. I became the only American missionary living with three other very capable and worthy Japanese elders. Needless to say I felt very inadequate. Nevertheless, with their love and support, we all fared very well. As far as the work was concerned nothing much changed except I had to pay the bills, hold meetings, and conduct interviews, etc.

Atypical to my character, on one particular day I decided that we should do some organizing and clean up around the apartment. We were going through some junky papers and old unopened mail when we came across something I had never seen before. It was a card from Salt Lake, some sort of referral card. It was one of those cards that tourists fill out when they come to the Visitor's Center at Temple Square in Salt Lake City, if they want to learn more about the Church. Honda-san was one such tourist.

The cards from Salt Lake are in turn, sent on to missionaries nearest to where the person resides. This card had been among a stack of other random papers in our apartment, for who knows how long. Nakamura and I decided to take a quick bike ride to look into it. Upon reaching the address, we were able to meet Honda-san. She explained that she had been traveling in the States and was just passing through Salt Lake. She and her fellow travelers decided it would be interesting to check out Temple Square and joined the tour at the Visitor's Center. Apparently she was so impressed with the presentation that she felt compelled to fill out the above mentioned card.

By the time we found her, I think she had already given up on ever being visited. Very quickly we began the lessons and continued teaching her until I was transferred.

Dear Grandma,

I was going along thinking that I had answered your letter when I didn't. All the while I was waiting for your letter. I feel pretty stupid. I'm sorry! So many things have been

happening here that I get all wrapped up in it and forget the real world.
We are still teaching a lot. I'm looking at 3 more baptisms. But I'll probably get transferred first.
Today is the first P-day we've had in the last 3 months where we didn't have an appointment. It's not that we're all that busy; it's just that investigators like to hear the Gospel on Monday.
It's starting to cool off now. We're wearing our suits in the evenings. I have a feeling that this year's winter will be cold, but I'm ready this time!
I've made some incredible friends here. I'm going to hate to go. But if I do, that's okay.
Take care and believe me when I say how much I love you.

Pete

On transfer day we usually waited around in the apartment for a call from the Buch, just in case. Up to this point, I had only been in other areas for a couple of months, three at the most. But I had been in Omuta for going on six months. For the last couple of those months, I had expected to get a transfer call. So I wasn't too surprised when the call finally did come. I would be heading northward to Ijiri. Although I wasn't shocked at the call, my heart began breaking at the thought of leaving what I considered my home in the mission.

My new companion would be Elder Hall from Texas. I would have to get used to being with an American companion all over again. I was truly, truly sad to say goodbye to my dear companion, Nakamura Choro. Nevertheless, that long anticipated day would be busier than ever. I had a lot of people to say goodbye to, and I only had one day in which to do it. Immediately, I packed up my stuff so I could free up the rest of the day. In my journal entry I wrote:

> Got up. Tenkin Happyo (transfer announcement)… Morris Choro Ijiri ni tenkin shimasu (Elder Morris you are to be transferred to Ijiri). Oh crud… here we go. Packed. Called Yamashita Shimai… She came over. Went out to Tomoko's house… said goodbye to her mom and dad. Went to the hospital to see Umezawa-san (Mr. Umezawa had been in the hospital for the past week.) Went to Arao Koko (Arao High School) to say goodbye to the class. Then to Hiroshima's… then to Yamshita's. Back for 6 minutes and back to Tachibana… said goodbye but they will come tomorrow. Went to Kinoshita's then Ikegami's… then to Eikaiwa (English class)… starting to feel it all. Went to Kajihara's then to

Umezawa's. Went to the Doi's for Yakiniku… then home. Honda-san called. Bed.

The final stop that night was "the Doi's". The Doi family was a very special family in the branch and to me in particular. Their daughter Takami had a special sprit about her. Although her family had not been in the Church very long, Takami was one of our best member-missionaries. During my whole time in Omuta, she introduced the Gospel to nearly all of her close friends at school. We taught a couple of them and later on, at least one joined the Church. Takami's parents were also a delight. They owned a barber shop. I had mentioned earlier that most beauty salons and barber shops were closed on Monday but were open on Sunday.

Brother and sister Doi worked as partners in their shop. Due to the nature of their work, they were not able to attend church on Sunday. Yet, showing faith, they made a point to close their business on the first Sunday of each month so they could attend. I will never forget the kindness of the Doi family. Not just because they gave the missionaries free haircuts, but because they were a loving and faithful family.

There were still a number of people that I never got to say goodbye to before transfer day. We came home quite late that evening. It was one of the saddest days of my entire mission thus far. I should at least follow up on the Umezawa Family at this point.

Since we had begun teaching Chiyo and her mother, we had taught the entire lesson plan, twice in some parts. We were confident that both Chiyo and her mother were very close to joining the Church, as they had become very receptive to the lessons. They were reading the Book of Mormon as well as attending Church. By the time I was transferred, we were visiting them at least twice a week. Going to their house was like being in my own home, and the Spirit was very strong there. The night before I transferred, I was compelled to tell them that I was not going to beat around the bush with them anymore.

"You know these things are true." I said. Both Chiyo and her mom could not deny it. I knew that they were ready to be baptized, so I said it straight away, "You need to be baptized and I know that you know it". We all shed tears as Chiyo's mother instantly said that she wanted to be baptized. My heart was pounding as I turned to Chiyo for her reply. Awkwardly, she replied, "I don't think I'm ready right now; but that doesn't mean I will never join the Church; I'm just not ready." Regardless of what Chiyo said, I received a witness that they would both be baptized very soon. I was also glad that at least this time, I had the courage to follow the Spirit and make the challenge.

I was absolutely overwhelmed at the number of people that came to see me off on a regular week day. I won't even try to name names. Some took time off from work or missed school to come to the train station. I was surprised at the amount of liquid my tear ducts could produce. I felt a terrible hole developing in my heart. It was like leaving home all over again.

Coincidentally, Honda-san would be traveling in the same direction as I, so we boarded the train together. I continued to correspond with nearly everybody that I left behind in Omuta during my remaining months in Japan. I have since been back to visit and still have a tender spot in my heart for that place.

Chapter 10: Back to the City

I arrived at the train station near Ijiri and was greeted by the whole gang from my new district. Ijiri is a district within the very large city of Fukuoka. My companion, Elder Hall and I hit it off very quickly. He had a laid back nature about him; perhaps it was the Texas in him. He would be my first American companion that was not from Utah. The sister missionaries were also there, including my dear friend from way back in Kagoshima, Sister Kunugi.

Sister Kunugi and I had been in contact all along the way. Nearly each time that I was transferred, she would call to see how I was doing. I was so happy to see her again. The Zone Leaders were also in the crowd. We would be in the same apartment. First there was Takahori Choro, who we all ended up calling just "Tak". You can imagine my surprise when I laid eyes on his companion. It was none other than my very best friend in the mission, Elder Stoneman. It's true; together once again. Right away, I began to imagine what sorts of mischief the little borough of Ijiri was in store for.

As it was with my other transfers, Elder Hall and I didn't waste any time at all. After settling in and a quick planning meeting, we taught a lesson that very night. When we returned, I was bombarded by a plethora of calls from Omuta. Everyone wanted to make sure that I had arrived okay.

From day one, Elder Hall and I kept pretty busy with our existing investigators. We seemed to have something going on every night. After such a long stretch in the countryside, the city brought on many new challenges for me. Our bike riding style was much different than in Omuta. Elder Nakamura would never have approved of our speed. It was pretty crazy, possibly even dangerous.

I don't remember dealing with such busy traffic in any other area. On our second night, Elder Hall went to battle with a minivan. On the way out to our lesson, we came upon some road construction. Cones had been set out to gradually merge the traffic over into the inside lane. We were rapidly running out of road to ride on. In order to safely merge with the cars, we would have to increase our speed. One particular driver of a minivan refused to make room for us and began to force Hall Choro off the road. I couldn't believe my eyes and it still makes me laugh when I think about it. Thinking back, it is possible that the driver wasn't even aware of Hall's presence.

Frantically pedaling, Hall began pounding his fist on the side of the van as it continued to veer toward him. Seeing Hall's situation, I didn't even bother merging; I eventually came to a halt amongst the cones. Hall ultimately ended up riding through the cones as well. I was laughing so hard that I fell over with my bike. I am not sure how, but we still made it to our appointment on time, relatively unscathed.

The apartment in Ijiri was situated more squarely in the city than I had ever been thus far in my mission. Our area crossed and blended with several other areas, including the Hombu. Being so close, we often ran into Hombu missionaries, including the Buch himself.

In the countryside there was hardly anything to do besides the work. But the city seemed to bring on many more distractions. We became pretty frequent lunchtime customers at Shakey's Pizza. The pizza was made pretty much the same as back home, and for just a few hundred yen, they had a TABEHODAI or "all you can eat buffet". They served the standard pepperoni and sausage pizzas, which were usually devoured by the missionaries as soon as they were put out. But right up there with some of the strangest things I ever saw in Japan were the other pizzas that were available. I never would have imagined eating corn pizza, squid pizza, or a few others that I couldn't even identify.

On one particular P-day, the four of us headed down to Shakey's. As we began to eat, we noticed through the window that the elders from the Hombu were about to come in. Of course they were the envy of the mission; they always went around in cars instead of bikes. They were parking their car on the street in front of the restaurant. Following behind them was the Buch in his own car. Apparently the street in front was designated a "No Parking" zone. Nevertheless, both cars were parked there. It wasn't but a minute or two before a policeman came along.

We watched as the officer first stopped to peer into the car of the very American looking elders. They conversed for a short while; the officer just shook his head and moved on to the Buch's car. Then the officer and the Buch spent a little while conversing, but then the Buch drove away. It appeared that the elders may have intentionally spoken poor Japanese, which frustrated the officer into giving up. The officer then moved on to the Buch's car. Although President Shimizu was also an American, his very Japanese face didn't help much in getting any slack from Fukuoka's finest; he was forced to find another place to park. I have to admit, the "I don't speak Japanese" tactic comes in handy once in a while for me as well.

Stoneman and I picked up where we had left off before. We always managed to find new ways to entertain ourselves. Besides Shakey's there were other popular places for us to go and eat without busting the bank. Back in Omuta, Nakamura Choro and I had discovered an out of the way little restaurant. It was just an old couple operating it; but I can tell you that to this day, I have yet to find a better KATSUDON (breaded pork cutlet over rice, topped with egg and onions and a sweet soy based sauce). That was the last thing we ate for lunch the day before I left. Here in the city, was a chain restaurant called "Gyoza no

Osho" (King of the Potstickers). They had the best menu, suited perfectly for missionaries… cheap and large portions. Their specialty was gyozas (pot stickers), but they had other great things on the menu as well.

We frequented Osho's two or more times a week. The location we liked the most had seating for about ten or twelve people along a bar facing the kitchen… a one-man operation. We became quite familiar with the chef and sometimes he would sneak in a few freebies. Our favorite thing was watching him at the wok. If he was cooking the right stuff, he could get the flames to go straight to the ceiling. I remember one of us ordering sautéed liver just to see the show.

Stoneman had become quite intrigued with cooking himself, and would often attempt to emulate the dishes we enjoyed at Osho's. One time he tried to get the chef to divulge the recipe for the sauce in a dish called TENSHIN HAN, another of our favorites. It was a light colored creamy sauce with a distinct flavor. The chef said that he could get in trouble if he were to ever give out the recipe, but he did give us a small sample to take home. I remember how Stoneman labored to match up that taste with his own concoction of ingredients. I must say he did manage to come very close to the real thing.

I had transferred to Ijiri about a week before Thanksgiving. The holidays didn't help much in keeping the time from flying by. While we were busy with holiday activities, we were just as busy teaching and finding investigators. The city brought on a new twist to finding new investigators. Growing up, I had never encountered the dynamics of a big city. An occasional trip to Seattle was the extent of my experience. We found and became good friends with a wide variety of people here in Fukuoka.

One day as we were walking along in a semi-outdoor mall, a voice called out to us, "GAIJIN-SAN". "GAIJIN-SAN" (Mr. Foreigner), which was a common form of address used in Japan for the American missionaries. I think today, more and more Japanese people believe that term to be somewhat rude, so I don't here it much anymore. We looked around to see who was hailing us, but there was no one to be found. As we started to move along, the call came again, "Gaijin-san". Upon further inspection, we saw two young men hidden inside a tiny sushi shop, motioning for us to come in. They had big grins on their faces and seemed excited to see us.

Inside the shop we could see that, as there were no customers, they were busy cleaning up. We soon learned that they were brothers. The elder of the two was seventeen and his brother was fifteen. We further learned that they had left home and were living on their own, working at this sushi shop. The elder boy, Yuki was an apprentice to become a sushi chef and his brother worked cleaning and serving. The boss was out, so they offered to make us some free sushi. Yuki was very skilled at his new trade, from what we could see. We soon became friends with these kids and visited them often.

We also managed to begin visiting the family of one of our students from the English class. Her name was Miho. She invited us out to her house after class one day. We arrived there to find that her house was attached to the family business, yet another sushi shop. Apparently, she had already planned on bringing us home, because her dad didn't seem surprised to see us. In fact he had us belly up to the counter, ready to make us anything we wanted. It's a good thing I had gotten over my sushi phobia early on, or I would have been in trouble in this area.

As soon as we hit the month of December, we were absolutely swamped. Out of the blue a dear sweet sister from the branch back in Futsukaichi called our apartment when she learned that Stoneman and I were together again. She asked if we would be interested in coming to the hospital where her daughter was being cared for; she wanted us to come and sing Christmas carols there. It so happened that there was an old and broken guitar in our apartment. After a few days of scrounging around for the necessary parts, I managed to fix it up. Back home, I was often the accompanist during Christmas time. I had never taken any real lessons, but could fake it pretty well.

At the hospital, in addition to the singing, I was also asked to be Santa Clause there. Although I was the smallest of the bunch, playing Santa sounded kind of fun. That morning we practiced a number of songs, and then met up with the two other elders from Futsukaichi. Upon arrival, we learned that we would be singing in a hospital ward comprised of severely disabled children. When we entered the room, it seemed that many of the kids were not even aware of what was going on; but it was very clear that their parents were extremely grateful to have us come. We knew that the sister's daughter was there, but for some reason she wasn't among the children in the room. As we sang our songs, everyone was smiling and happy, in spite of how bad we may have sounded. It then became time for me to change into the oversized Santa suit that had been prepared for me.

It was never actually explained to me just what my job as Santa would entail, until just before I put on the suit. Apparently, all the parents had brought presents for their own children beforehand. My job would be to simply deliver each family's present to the corresponding child. On the surface, that may not seem too difficult a task, but as I began to pass out the gifts, I was overcome with the Spirit. I had never before been put in such a situation. Quite frankly, I was a little scared as to how to act; or how I would be received by not only these severely debilitated kids, but also by their parents. As it would turn out, I was unexpectedly blessed with something very special that day.

As I looked into the eyes of each child, I could somehow sense the perfect beauty of their very spirits.

Tears of joy appeared in the eyes of the parents who, to me, were paragons of unconditional love. Although it seemed to us that many of the children could hardly comprehend a single thing; each parent treated their little one the same as if there was no handicap at all.

I could not hold back the tears; and frankly, I didn't even try. I had to blink each time before moving to the next child, so I could read the name on the tag. Even now, each time I read the seventeenth chapter of Third Nephi, I remember that scene at the hospital. I was so overcome by the Spirit that perhaps I cried as Jesus must have.

I was blessed for a moment to see, through my spiritual eyes, the very essence of those little children. In my heart I wanted to declare to the parents as Jesus did, "Behold your little ones."[31] After our time with the kids, we learned where that kind sister's daughter had been. It turned out that she was too incapacitated to join the others and was bedridden. Nevertheless, we spent a little time with her and her mother afterwards. A couple of weeks later I put on another Santa suit at the preschool of another ward member's child. In yet a different way, I felt the Spirit through those wonderful little kids.

---

[31] 3 Nephi 17: 23

Without reservation, I would have to say that this was the most wonderful and meaningful Christmas I had ever had.

The day after our hospital visit, the call came that Stoneman was being transferred. The previous night, he had pulled me aside to tell me what he had done. Paraphrasing, I think he told me that being a ZL just wasn't his cup of tea. He just wanted to go back to being a regular missionary, whose worries involved only the basic of missionary work. He would have rather spent his time tracting and teaching than worrying about managing a bunch of other missionaries and dealing with all their problems. I must say that even in the short time that I was around Stoneman, I saw my share of the type of problems that can, and often do occur.

I understood how Stoneman felt, but I must admit that I was a little disheartened. While I didn't care too much about being a ZL either, I do confess that the thought had crossed my mind about being one with Stoneman. I didn't have much time left and thought it would be a good way to finish up my mission. That would have made a cool ending to this story, don't you think? But as I have learned, there truly is a reason for everything.

I didn't know at the time, but there were other things that the Lord had in store for me, before I would be heading home. Once again, I found myself saying goodbye to my good friend Stoneman. We spoke on the phone over the next few months; I can attest to the fact that he was indeed happier. Later on, he even found a way to get transferred to my favorite place, Omuta.

I had kept in contact with many of the good friends I had met along the way. The Umezawas called a couple times a week. Sister Koga from Futsukaichi kept in touch as well. And occasionally, Mr. Chuman (Yasuyuki's dad) from Kagoshima would check up on me too. A few of the teenagers from my English class in Omuta also kept in touch, and even came to visit during the New Year's holiday. Christmastime was hard that year, but in a different way than the year before. I was homesick for family back home last year. But this year, I was sad that I couldn't be around all the family I had accumulated in Japan.

Besides the Santa gigs, we were busy in a lot of other ways. The Christmas Zone Conference was a two-day affair. On the first day we gathered to do skits, watched Christmas videos and opened presents. The second day was a testimony meeting. The Buch gave a particularly moving talk. I paid a little closer attention to him this time because I was asked to translate for the Japanese missionaries. There was a lot of emotion expressed in the testimonies borne that day.

New Years was even busier. Like the year before, we had some extra time on our hands because everyone was too busy to see us. I mentioned the short visit from my former English students. The Umezawa family came up to see me as well. They took Elder Hall and me to an amusement park and spoiled us with a lot of food and presents. As it was not too far, Chiyo and her mom had already come up once before for lunch during December.

On New Year's morning, Sister Koga called and asked if we wanted to go for a drive with her family. We ended up going all the day long. By the end of that day, we had ridden a ferry, walked up a soon to erupt active volcano[32], and unwittingly traveled through three zones in the mission. Before we knew it, it had become nighttime. In fact, we had completely forgotten that a young sister had invited us to their house for a New Year's party that evening. We tried to make up for it by watching a bowl game with them the next day. She was pretty mad. Sorry Ikuko Shimai.

I should probably back up to what had happened New Year's Eve. After visiting a few members' homes, we received a call from one of our families. Earlier I told you about Miho, who lives at the sushi restaurant. Her dad called to invite us to usher in the New Year with the family. The missionaries had already gotten permission from the Buch to stay out after midnight; so we expected to have an especially fun night. When we arrived at Miho's house, everyone seemed so busy.

Although they were closed for business, Miho's dad was behind the counter cleaning his

---

[32] The volcano referred to is Mt. Unzen in Nagasaki Prefecture. In 1991 an eruption killed 44 people and changed the landscape significantly.

knives, etc. Inside the house, the mom was washing the wooden floor. They told us that Miho and her sister were doing their homework and we could hang out with them until the food was ready. As a missionary, I paid little attention to the fact that Miho was, let's just say, somewhat mature for her young fifteen-year-old age. It almost felt like the whole thing was set up as a joke by the parents to put us in a semi-awkward situation. Nothing against the rules ever happened, but it just felt a bit uncomfortable. I can admit now that Miho was very cute, and would have been attractive to just about any young man; so we soon removed ourselves back to where the adults were.

Being around Miho's parents was almost as uncomfortable, because they were so busy at work. The only alternative for us was to offer to pitch in and help. In no time we found ourselves mopping the floor of the restaurant. Later we were folding napkins, labeling chopsticks, and filling tiny fish-shaped plastic bottles with soy sauce.

Finally, at about ten minutes to twelve, the mom called everybody into the living room. On TV, we all watched a live program where a group of very old monks were climbing a mountain to a small shrine. One of them began ringing a huge iron bell as the clock struck midnight. Then everybody began yelling "AKEMASHITA OMEDETOU GOZAIMASU" (Happy New Year). Just then, the mom jumped up and began serving the food that she had previously been preparing; we immediately began to feast. In the meantime, Miho managed to meander her way next to where I was seated on the floor. For a couple of minutes, Hall just laughed at me in my plight. At last, he came over and put himself between us. To my relief, she backed off. All in all it was an interesting evening. We actually did have fun in spite of the slightly weird stuff.

A couple of days later, the Buch came to our apartment for a visit. After he met with the ZLs, he wanted to give me an interview. No, it didn't have anything to do with New Year's Eve at Miho's house. He told me that he wanted to transfer me in the next couple of days. I don't remember even being surprised. I had already told him in a letter that I felt the same way as Stoneman, just wanting to finish up my mission by working hard.

The Buch explained that my new companion was a good missionary, but wasn't quite ready to become a senior; in spite of the fact that he had passed off with an AP. He just needed a little extra mentoring. I was a little befuddled as to how to react. I wasn't so sure this was how I wanted to finish up my mission, seeing that I only had a little over two months left. I suppose I may have seen it as a babysitting job. Nevertheless, I accepted the challenge, and it would turn out to be exactly that.

Chapter 11: Last Stop: Fujisaki

Leaving Ijiri turned out to be somewhat uneventful. Nevertheless, I would miss Elder Hall. The elders from the Hombu came by and drove me to my new area in the same Hombu van that brought me from the airport when I first arrived. I neglected to mention that I already had a few preconceived ideas about my new companion. Stoneman called me many months before, when he was assigned to be his trainer back in Futsukaichi, after his first greenie, Elder Walton was transferred. Stoneman related to me that this young man was not much of a people person, and tended to be a little self-centered. Stoneman shared more of his idiosyncrasies as their time together passed. With the new assignment, this knowledge led me to believe that working with him wasn't going to be easy.

On our first day, we spent time getting to know each other while shopping for supplies. I actually found him to be quite pleasant, deciding that he must have grown out of whatever I had heard about him. We found a common interest watching a little college bowl football on TV at the local electronics store on P-day. We had a number of investigators that were at different stages of the lesson plan; so we had a lesson almost every night.

Things seemed to be going pretty well in this new area. It was fun to be reunited with

Elder Thomas from my MTC group. I think this was the first time seeing him since we first arrived. Elder Bellows was his companion… still a little green. He had very blonde hair, so we had fun addressing him with a number of nicknames, (Billy Idol, Brian Adams, Whitey, etc.). I began to think that this place might not be so bad after all. But as my first instincts tried to tell me, it didn't even take a week before my new companion and I began seeing things a little differently.

The arguments between my companion and I were usually over very trivial things. He started to come off as very critical about everything we did. Exactly one week from my arrival, I was ready to call it quits and ask to be transferred. On our one week anniversary, I wrote in my planner:

> Up.. studied.. slept.. got up and ate.. fudded (bathed). Went to MDM then to Osho's. Then went out with Bellows. Told Thomas the deal "That's it!" (I had enough with this companion) Went to Ohori Park and did street for a while. Met Masashi and his girlfriend. Went to his house and taught him a bit. Back.. Bed.

Thomas happened to be the DL there and I told him how hard it was for me to find middle ground with this new companion of mine. He told me that he would talk to the Buch and see what he could do. I began to understand why this young man was having so much trouble becoming a senior.

Soon after I arrived, my companion wanted to go out and buy a tennis racket. I hadn't seen any other rackets in the apartment and wondered who it was that he was planning to play with. That next morning I understood his plan as we were awakened by a repetitive thumping sound. Although it was still dark outside, I could see that my companion was not in his futon. I followed the thumping sounds to the outside and down the stairs. As I approached, I discovered what the sound was.

I found my companion in the apartment parking lot, hitting a tennis ball against the side of the apartment building. It wasn't against our apartment wall, because we were on the second floor. He was banging the ball on the outside wall of our downstairs neighbor… at 5:30 AM. What's even more unbelievable is that he was surprised and even angry, that I would dare tell him to stop. It was clear then, that we were in for a long haul together.

My frustration eventually came to a head the following Sunday. That night, we had an appointment to give a lesson, which my companion had prepared. When we arrived, the investigator informed us that something had come up and they would have to cancel. My companion got steaming mad, and then blamed me.

As a result of Thomas' intervention, the next morning we received a very timely call from the Buch. Within an hour, we were sitting in the Buch's office, each telling our own side of the story. I suppose I expected a little more understanding from the Buch during our interview. I thought for sure he would make arrangements to move either myself, or my companion somewhere else. No such luck; after he interviewed both of us separately, he brought us together again for a lecture on how to get along. Then the Buch put us on our knees, and we all prayed. First the Buch prayed, and then we each prayed for guidance. The Buch prayed that the Lord might provide a way for us to come together.

Oddly enough, I was actually able to see the picture in a different light from that moment. I'm not sure what kind of confirmation we got there in the Buch's office, but as soon as we got home, my companion came down with a very nasty sickness. In fact, for the next week and a half, all of us in the apartment came down with it as well. This was definitely not the answer that I was looking for, but it would turn out to be somewhat of a temporary distraction. Soon, something more dramatic would happen that forced us to come together once and for all.

Each morning, the four of us dragged our lazy bones out of our futons and gathered to study in a small common room. This day was no different from any other day. It was about 5:45 and the rain was coming down in sheets outside. I was sitting in a beat up old reclining chair with my back to the window. The others were sprawled out under a low table on the floor. We all had our scriptures propped up as if we were studying, but more likely had our eyes shut. I can't be too sure about the others because I believe that mine were. The noise from the rain was loud, almost hypnotic.

Just as I began studying, above the sound of the rain I heard a faint metallic clanking sound outside. It was loud enough to catch my attention, but apparently, no one else had noticed it. I did my best to ignore it, but something told me that I should look outside. So with a slight protest from the others, I opened the window. Outside the window, I could see the dike of the river with a small road on the top of the embankment. As I strained my eyes through the rain and darkness, I began to see strangely shaped silhouettes on the road. It looked as though someone may have fallen from their bicycle; I could hear a faint voice calling out.

Within seconds, my companion and I were running out the door in our bare feet. I barely had time to throw my overcoat on over my pajamas. We sloshed our way up the muddy bank to find a very disturbing scene. It actually looked as though there had been a two bicycle collision. I know that may sound somewhat odd, but what we saw was pretty shocking. Apparently, in the dark and wet conditions, two unsuspecting people had managed to blindly yet perfectly collide head-on into each other. I can't even imagine what the odds would be for both front tires to line up with such exactness.

The victims of the accident were a tiny middle-aged woman on her way to an early morning job and a six foot, one-hundred and fifty pound teenager on his way to school. Both of them were still on the ground; the boy was just starting to get up, but the woman was still laid out on the pavement. As we got closer, we could see that the woman had essentially flown over the handlebars. By the looks of it, she didn't even have time to break her fall. She had landed directly on her face.

The woman's body seemed to be slightly convulsing; her face still fixed against the asphalt. Thinking that she might have a neck injury, we were hesitant to move her head. Yet in the dim light, we could see that blood was pooling around her face. We were scared, to say the least. The boy was crying and screaming that it was his fault and that he had killed her. I gingerly turned her head to one side, allowing for an airway, but she didn't appear to be breathing very well.

Suddenly, the boy passed out and fell backwards down the slick, muddy bank. I glanced up to see that Thomas and Bellows were peering out of the apartment window; so as I ran to help the boy I shouted," Call an ambulance!" Thomas waived his hand in compliance. It must have been the adrenaline rush, but somehow I managed to hoist that big boy onto my shoulder and carry him back up to the top. When I returned, the woman continued to struggle just to get a good breath. We weren't sure what more we could do. Without a single word, my companion and I made eye contact. Simultaneously, we fell on our knees and put our hands on her head. With a nod from my companion, by the power of the priesthood, I gave her a desperate blessing.

To our amazement, no sooner than we said our amens, her body seemed to calm, and she began breathing almost normally. It was surreal. My companion then put his coat over her rain-soaked body.

The situation seemed to be somewhat stabilized, so I ran inside to grab some blankets. When I entered the apartment, Thomas was still on the phone. "What's the word for ambulance?" he yelled. Perhaps you might recall the incident back in Futsukaichi? When that man was lying hurt on the train tracks… That was the first time I had used the word KYUKYUSHA (ambulance). This was more than a year later. I was a little surprised that Thomas, who had come to Japan on the same plane as me, hadn't already learned that all important word. I quickly blurted out the answer and dashed back out the door with nearly all the bed blankets. I scurried up the bank and put them over the woman and the boy.

A warm feeling of relief came over me when the ambulance finally drove away. I was sure that the woman and the boy were going to be okay. My companion and I had experienced something very special that day. Looking back now, I know in my heart that the Buch, through inspiration, may have known something like this might happen. We were of one heart that day. All our differences were wiped away as we knelt over that woman.

The remaining time that we had together was actually pretty enjoyable. There wasn't much time left before I would be going home. I think that if we could have spent it together, we might very well have seen more great things happen. But I knew in my heart that my companion was ready to move on as a senior. Sure enough, he would be called away five days later.

The story of the bike wreck didn't end on that narrow river road. The boy and his mother came by our apartment a couple of days later to thank us by offering some money and a cake. She said that the money was to pay for the cleaning of our blankets. I told the mother that we would gladly eat the cake, but she could keep her money. Nevertheless, she was very adamant and insisted on giving it to us. I told her that if she was willing to meet us at the Church building on Sunday, there would be a person who could take the money as a donation. She happily agreed. My new companion and I met the boy and his mom two weeks later at the church, where they met our Bishop. He received the money and explained how it would be utilized. The mother seemed very pleased. I then gave them a Book of Mormon. The boy promised to read it.

The next few weeks flew by faster than I could have ever imagined. We were very busy with mission, ward, and stake conferences. I was able to see many of the friends that I had made along the way. I also had the privilege of translating for the Buch one last time at our zone conference. My new companion, Nobuhara Choro and I tried to keep our investigator pool alive. We also managed to give out several *Books of Mormon*.

During Christmastime back in Ijiri, I had been looking at the possibility of extending my mission. I was all geared up to tell my parents of my intentions during the Christmas call home. I knew that both my parents had been working extra hours to keep me on my mission. I certainly didn't want to add to the burden. Nevertheless, when I began to tell them my feelings about the matter, they both became a little uneasy. That was when my dad went ahead and spilled the beans.

It turned out that my parents had been scrimping to put aside enough money to come to Japan and bring me home. I knew that this was a big deal for them. They weren't able to do this for the other brothers. My head started to spin. I thought I had made my mind up about staying, but at the same time I became excited at the prospect of showing my parents the country that I had truly come to love. Not wanting to spoil my parents' surprise, I was happy to resolve to go home as planned. It suddenly became more and more difficult to write home; I didn't want to cloud my mind with the thoughts of going home so soon.

Dear Pete,

We haven't heard from you for a couple of weeks and I'm beginning to wonder if everything is okay with you. When we talked on the phone, I got the feeling that you might be a little down but our excitement about the trip didn't let me explore if it were true or not. I haven't as yet found out how you really feel about our coming…

Dad

I know that my parents were concerned about my emotions. I could have stayed in Japan indefinitely, if that were at all possible. But one has to move on with his or her real life at some point.

Dear Pete,

…Dad and I have done a great deal of thinking on this… We have several reasons for feeling this way…
I know how much you love your mission and how much you love learning the language and for this reason would probably love to stay. However Dad and I feel it would be wise for you to come home after the time you contracted for…

We love you and miss you very much.
Love you a whole bunch,

Mom

I finally came to grips that my mission would come to an end. Besides, what better way to show my parents what I had done and how much I loved Japan than to show them first hand? Despite all the distractions, we somehow managed to get a young man that we had been teaching to accept a baptismal challenge.

I received a plethora of calls each night from all over the 14,114 square miles that made up Kyushu Island. Mr. Chuman, Yasuyuki's dad back in Kagoshima called me three or four times during that month. On the last call, he broke down and cried; so did I. Brother and Sister Koga from Futsukaichi called a number of times as well, and we ended up at their house for dinner three nights before I went home. Sister Inada's family from Kumamoto called a few times too. But the majority of the calls of course came from Omuta. Chiyo Umezawa and her parents called me every few days. Many of the members there called as well. It got harder and harder as the day to leave loomed nearer.

I got to see Stoneman one last time when I went for my exit interview with the Buch. He was probably picking up yet another greenie, or something. We talked for a short while, exchanged hugs, and then off he went again. The Hombu had kindly made arrangements to coordinate with my parents' itinerary. I would be leaving on a Sunday, flying out of Fukuoka to meet them at the Narita (Tokyo) airport.

The day before leaving, I had done things as if it were any other day. I conducted my English class; we went out to work a little, and then came home. That night, I made dozens of phone calls thanking people and saying my goodbyes. My emotions were so twisted up that I didn't know how to express my feelings very well.

My very last day in the field was an indescribably strange day, almost dreamlike. I was already packed up when a kind member of the ward picked me up and took me to the Yakuin chapel. That was where the Hombu missionaries attended Sunday services. During Sunday School, the APs transported me to the airport. Without any fanfare, I was cordially dropped off at the doors at the airport entrance… alone. And that was exactly how I felt, alone. It was as though I had been stripped of all my protection. For the first time since the MTC I was suddenly missing the shadow of a companion. My thoughts were going in every direction.

I made my way to the ticket counter and checked in my baggage. I suppose I was feeling a little depressed; perhaps I was thinking I deserved a better sendoff as I started up the escalator. To my amazement and surprise, I was greeted at the top by a fairly large crowd, waiting to see me off. Some of them had traveled considerable distances to be there for me. My heart soared at their generosity and the sacrifices made to give me such a farewell.

The night before, others had expressed their desire to come, which also warmed my heart. It was hard to part over the phone. There wasn't much time to spend with my friends there at the boarding area. I felt bad that they had gone so far out of their way. They said their final goodbyes, leaving me with several small tokens of their love. Soon I was at the gate and on the plane. The plane was not very full and I easily found my seat by the window. Actually there were no passengers near to where I was seated.

Sitting in my seat awaiting take off, my mind began to clear. You know how it has been said that just before a person dies, their whole life passes before their eyes. I was clearly on the brink of death, the end of my mission. I began to review my time in Japan from the very moment I met little Chihiro Nakazawa on the plane coming to Japan.

I thought about all my companions and the literally hundreds of people that I had the blessing and privilege to contact. This caused me to wonder, "Did I really make a difference?"; "Was I a good missionary? To this day I lament the time that I surely wasted while I was in the mission field. I know I could have worked a little harder, knocked on a few more doors, or taught a little better.

As the plane made its way onto the

tarmac and commenced to prime its engines for takeoff, I began to sob. I kept my face fixed outside the porthole of a window to hide my weeping face from possible onlookers. My heart began to break as I was forced to say goodbye to a life that I had truly come to love. As we rose up into the clouds, I watched the city fade away until I couldn't make out any of its features. When I met my parents in Tokyo, I cried some more with the joy of being reunited with my loved ones; yet also the sadness knowing that being in their arms meant that it really was over.

Epilogue

A few years ago, I received an e-mail from a dear friend who happens to live in Omuta. She had also been a missionary in the Fukuoka Mission some years after I had left. We met through the alumni section of our mission website. Following her mission, she moved back to Japan and is currently married, living and working in Omuta. Some time prior to that e-mail, I was able to visit Omuta during a business trip. My friend and her kind husband offered to take me in during my stay there.

In this later e-mail, she told me of their latest Stake Conference in Kumamoto. She told me of a sister who had recently lost her husband to cancer. This sister gave a very moving talk, describing her last weeks with him. My friend then related to me how strong her testimony was; that her strength in the gospel will certainly sustain her through her trials. At last, she told me who this good sister was. To my surprise and amazement, she was none other than Chiyo Umezawa. I am sure you recall Chiyo… the young woman whose family had been labeled "DROPPED" in the area book; the one who made it very difficult for us to get back into their home. You might further recall that after much persistence, my companion and I were finally able to begin teaching the Gospel to Chiyo and her mother.

We had made much progress with them and by the time I was transferred, their testimonies had grown tremendously.

The evening before I was to be transferred, I gave them both the baptismal challenge. Chiyo's mother readily accepted the challenge. But once again, if you remember, Chiyo's response was, "I don't think I'm ready right now... but that doesn't mean I will never join the Church... I'm just not ready." I hadn't mentioned much more than the fact that I had kept in contact with the Umezawa Family, even after I had returned home.

Chiyo and her mother had come to visit me and my companion sometime around New Years after I had transferred. At that time I once again reiterated my challenge to her. Her response was much the same. But I was encouraged by her not dismissing baptism altogether. She said she simply wasn't ready.

A week or two passed, and I received a call from Chiyo. She was very quiet and her voice was quivering. When I asked her what the matter was she began to cry, confessing that she hadn't been all together truthful with me. She was just afraid of change. The fact of the matter was that she sincerely did want to be baptized and didn't want to wait any longer. Tears streamed down my cheeks as I tried hard not to jump up and down. Both she and her mom were ready to take this great step and join the fold of the Good Shepherd. To my surprise and sadness, Chiyo said that they both wanted for me to come and perform the ordinance. We all sobbed as I proceeded to tell them that I couldn't come back, due to zone restrictions in the mission.

Nevertheless, I insisted that they not wait and go ahead with their baptisms; I would call and make the arrangements. I hung up the phone and immediately called Elder Rogers, my replacement in Omuta, to tell him the wonderful news. I had known Elder Rogers for a short time in the MTC. "Merry Christmas", was the first thing I said. "Huh?" he replied. I went on to tell him that the Umezawas were ready to get baptized and all he needed to do is get the interviews out of the way… and fill up the font.

Chiyo was baptized in less than a month. Her mother was baptized soon after that. I had the opportunity to meet the Umezawas when I returned to Japan less than a year later and continued to correspond with them for some time after.

I was impressed with Chiyo's rapid progression as a member of the Church. Not long after joining, she was called to teach the Gospel Doctrine class in Sunday School. She eventually went on to serve in the Kobe, Japan mission. Upon her return, she was sealed to a return missionary in the temple of the Lord.

Now with Chiyo's husband having passed away at such a young age, she continues to raise their three boys on her own, one of which lives with severe autism. Not long after learning of her situation, I was able to rekindle my connection with Chiyo; she has related her testimony to me of the importance of the saving ordinances of the temple. As a missionary, I was privileged to bare my testimony to Chiyo and her mother countless times as they moved closer to joining the Savior's flock in Japan. Now Chiyo's testimony strengthens me.

In the Book of Mormon, we read of Ammon and his mission.[33] Growing up, like many young men, I loved to read of how Ammon, as a servant of the king, protected the royal flocks from evil men whose intensions were to scatter them. Almost every young man admires the way Ammon lopped off the arm of each man who raised his club to strike him. Today, it is so much easier for me to see an even deeper meaning to that story. Ammon had taken a personal interest in protecting his master's flocks, while the other servants were ready to flee; it was only he who understood just how important those flocks were to his king. To me, there is a profound meaning in the way he and his fellow servants went out into the fields. Even with the threat of those evil men lurking, those young men gathered the scattered sheep, bringing them together once again at the "place of water".

In my mind, that water represents the very living water of our Savior, the same water that Jesus offered to the woman at the

[33] Alma 17: 26-39

well[34]. We cannot let fear drive us from our duty, as it did with Ammon's companions. Missionaries have the responsibility and power to gather His scattered sheep… sheep that would continue to be lost if faithful servants did not step up and search for them in the service of their King. Every day, missionaries have the opportunity to bring these "scattered sheep" to the "place of water", escorting them to the comfort and safety of our Savior's loving arms.

Earlier, I likened our work on this earth to throwing a stone into the "proverbial pond of life" and that we may never see how far the ripples might have gone. I was given a great gift from our Heavenly Father to go out into the world and to teach His gospel. I did not choose where I was to go or who I was to contact. I was blessed to work as an instrument in His hands, in His time, and in His chosen place. I cannot presume to take much of the credit for what happened on my mission. Looking back, I can see that those "successes" were not exactly mine to claim.

The Lord, through the Spirit, was in charge during those times. I have to make that clear before I say anymore. I doubt that we will ever know just what the impact of finding someone like Chiyo Umezawa might be. The ripples from that "pond" are still forming. Who can say how many people might have been affected just by her serving a full time

[34] John 4: 5-14

mission. Chiyo's eldest son has since returned from his mission. I can only imagine how many more were affected by his testimony and will find the gospel through his service.

Before her son left on his mission, I received some wonderful news from Chiyo. Her brother's family had begun investigating the Church. As a result, Chiyo's brother and his four children were baptized. Nevertheless, my joy was even fuller when I more recently learned that the last hold out in the family, Chiyo's father had also made it to the waters of baptism.

Surely Chiyo's and Chiyo's mother's faith helped to bring about this miracle. I now envision the Umezawas at the altar of the temple to be sealed together for time and all eternity. How blessed I am to have been able to see some of the ripples in that pond during my lifetime, even three decades later. Three generations of Umezawas now play an active role within the Master's flock. I can't wait to hear the rest of the story as it continues to unfold. I smile when I think that there may be others like Yuka or Chiyo and her family to whom, as a missionary I had the privilege of sharing my testimony in Japan. If there are others, I look forward with the hope of meeting them once again either in this life or the next.

Let me just say once more what I said to those of you reading this story: Maybe there is a young man or woman out there who might be thinking, "How will my going on a mission make a difference to anything or anyone?" Again, I will say that you just never know. It might be many years later... But maybe, just maybe someone may walk up to you; look you in the eye and say, "Thank you for being there for me." On that wonderful day, imagine the joy that will be shared as you embrace each other as brothers or sisters in the gospel.

As a young man, I was given the task of caring for the little lamb Martha when she needed me; my dad delegated me with the duty of attending to her. I'm quite sure that he trusted me with this responsibility; but on occasion, there was certainly a need to be reminded of my duty. Dad soon chastened me when I shirked it. This duty undoubtedly caused me to have to sacrifice some of my own personal time. But I am sure that I grew from the experience. In the end, I felt the satisfaction and joy in the knowledge that little Martha would be able to return to the flock.

The Lord saw fit to send me 7,240 miles from my home to tend to His scattered sheep, His children in Japan. There were times when I needed reminding, even chastening in regards to what my duty was.

Nothing can compare to the joy that we all can feel from witnessing a person's mighty change of heart, and their desire to seek after the Savior. I will forever be grateful for the opportunity I was given to share my own testimony to those I met on my mission. That experience is the basis for my ability to share my belief of the divinity of our Savior and the truthfulness of His gospel today.

Over these many years I have come to understand that the testimonies we gain and hold sacred are essentially useless if we are not sharing them with the purpose of bringing others to the fold of the Master. Jesus asked Peter the seemingly simple question "Lovest thou me?" I am sure that many of us would have readily answered as Peter did, "Thou knowest that I love thee". The Savior's instruction to Peter, "feed my sheep", was not only Peter's, but also our mission call as well. No words can describe our duty more simply or clearly than those of the Savior's to Peter on the eve of His ultimate sacrifice:

"But I have prayed for thee, that thy faith fail not: and when thou art converted, strengthen thy brethren" Luke 22:32

www.ingramcontent.com/pod-product-compliance
Lightning Source LLC
Chambersburg PA
CBHW051822040426
42447CB00006B/322

* 9 7 8 0 6 1 5 9 0 8 8 2 3 *